Creating a Culture of Academic Integrity

A TOOLKIT FOR SECONDARY SCHOOLS

David B. Wangaard, Ed.D., and **Jason M. Stephens, Ph.D.**

SEARCH
INSTITUTE
PRESS

Credits
Book Design: Mighty Media
Production Supervisor: Mary Ellen Buscher

Library of Congress Cataloging-in-Publication Data
Wangaard, David B.
Creating a culture of academic integrity : a toolkit for secondary schools / David B. Wangaard, Jason M. Stephens.
     p.   cm.
  Includes bibliographical references and index.
  ISBN 978-1-57482-496-4 (pbk.)
  1. Cheating (Education)—United States—Prevention.
2. Education, Secondary—Moral and ethical aspects—United States. 3. School improvement programs—United States.
I. Stephens, Jason M. II. Title.
LB3609.W35 2011
373.15'8—dc22   2011007881

About Search Institute Press
Search Institute Press is a division of Search Institute, a nonprofit organization that provides catalytic leadership, breakthrough knowledge, and innovative resources to advance the health of children, youth, families, and communities. Our mission at Search Institute Press is to provide practical and hope-filled resources to help create a world in which all young people thrive. Our products are embedded in research, and the 40 Developmental Assets—qualities, experiences, and relationships youth need to succeed—are a central focus of our resources. Our logo, the SIP flower, is a symbol of the thriving and healthy growth young people experience when they have an abundance of assets in their lives.

CONTENTS

CHEATING, CULTURE, and CORE VALUES

CHAPTER 1

Understanding the Challenge

Let's begin with some numbers. According to our own research involving thousands of students at a diverse set of six high schools in the northeastern United States, as well as national surveys involving tens of thousands of high school students (e.g., Josephson Institute of Ethics 2009; McCabe 2008), more than 90 percent of students report engagement in at least one form of academic dishonesty each and every year.[1] Perhaps the most startling, and often overlooked, aspect of this epidemic is that most students report some form of cheating during a school year (an average of 95 percent in our study), while more than a majority (an average of 58 percent in our study) believe that cheating is morally wrong.

Thus, in addition to statistical reasons, the term *epidemic*, which has been used to characterize the problem since the mid-1980s (Haines, Diekhoff, LaBeff, and Clark 1986, p. 342), is appropriate because it associates academic dishonesty with illness. Like a disease, academic dishonesty has infected not only the validity of student learning and efforts to assess it, but also the development of our young people's integrity. In short, the epidemic of cheating creates three distinct types of problems: it undermines student learning, it invalidates assessment of that "learning," and it compromises student moral integrity and development.

It is for these reasons that we are deeply concerned about the epidemic of cheating and have spent the past decade working to understand the problem and design approaches to diminish it. This book is a toolkit for improving academic integrity. It represents a systematic, research-based approach that includes strategies that have been used in our *Achieving with Integrity* project.[2] As its name suggests, the primary goal of this project was to promote academic integrity and reduce cheating and plagiarism among high school students. A total of six high schools were recruited to participate in the project: three as participating or "pilot" schools and three as nonparticipating or "control" schools. All six were public schools in the northeastern United States: two served predominantly low-income, minority students; two predominantly mid-income, White students; and two predominantly high-income, White students.

Before introducing the organization of this toolkit, we want to make an important point about our perspective on the epidemic of cheating: namely, that we embrace, apply, and advocate a sociocultural perspective. Students today cheat more than students from previous decades;[3] this is not a result of some genetic mutation whereby children born in the 1990s are by nature more deviant/less moral than children born in the 1950s. Rather, the current epidemic of cheating is a product of a complex interplay of personal and environmental factors. Chief among these is our culture—its values, norms, goals, and so on—and the changes it has undergone over the past few decades.

Students themselves recognize the difference between historically stated norms of honesty and integrity and what is taking place in schools today. When provided the opportunity to anonymously comment on their school's administration of academic integrity policies, 20 percent of our student responders encouraged their school leaders to create or enforce stricter consequences for dishonesty (Wangaard and Stephens 2009). This theme represented the largest percentage of student responses.

Timely Drama

Students from the Joel Barlow High School (Redding, Connecticut) cast of *Richard Cory* were participating in the Connecticut Drama Association Festival. Part of the competition's rules for participation limited each drama team to 45 minutes of preparation time on stage before its presentation.

The Joel Barlow team was scheduled to present after lunch. Team members came back to the theater early and found the door open more than 60 minutes before their presentation. No one else was there. Their drama teacher was still at lunch. The students recognized the advantage this circumstance offered them. They could get onstage, arrange their props, and have extra time to practice before their scheduled presentation.

Upon reflection, the students understood that taking advantage of this "opportunity" would also violate the explicit 45-minute preparation time that all the other teams had prior to their presentations.

The Joel Barlow team chose to stay outside the theater until 45 minutes before its presentation.

Ashley Erickson, personal communication, March 30, 2010, to Catherine Correa, Redding, CT.

Students are put in a position to cheat by the administrators' emphasis on grades, test scores, and individual rankings. Good grades and CAPT scores supersede the intellectual health of students. The disintegration of the student to student and teacher to student confidentiality is what places students in situations where they feel they need to cheat if they wish to be successful. It is an issue which needs to be addressed at the administrator level.

High school student

In a world where life is often unfair and unjust we most often cheat our way to the top. Survival of the fittest is human nature and we all cheat when we see the opportunity and evaluate the level of sacrifice to cheat in the circumstance. I personally would cheat if I examined my surroundings and knew that my source was reliable and chances to be caught were very unlikely.

High school student

American Culture: Shifting Values and the Rise of Cheating

In his book *The Cheating Culture: Why More Americans Are Doing Wrong to Get Ahead*, David Callahan (2004) documents the shifts in moral values over the past several generations. Drawing on a wealth of statistics and stories, Callahan demonstrates how market values (such as self-interest, materialism, and greed) and a bottom-line economy have come to dominate the cultural landscape of America over the past 30 years. In doing so, he highlights an interesting or "ugly" paradox first articulated by the eminent sociologist Robert Merton: "A cardinal American virtue, 'ambition,' promotes a cardinal American vice, 'deviant behavior'" (quoted in Callahan 2004, p. 15). And in the United States, deviant behavior that results from monetary ambition is easily rationalized and rarely punished, particularly among those with wealth and power. While exceptions exist, white-collar crime often pays, and white-collar criminals are often treated leniently even when caught and convicted.

Our cultural indulgence of ambition does not escape the notice of our nation's youth. They see and understand that negative behavior exercised in pursuit of wealth, status, and power is a forgivable sin that is lightly punished, if at all. With this understanding in mind, how could the epidemic of cheating among our nation's youth be otherwise? In a culture saturated with corporate malfeasance, political scandals, and performance-enhancing drug use, how could our youth fail to resist the unethical (but far shorter) path to "success"? The answer is that they can't, or at least don't. For those who think the epidemic of cheating is primarily a problem among low achievers or the academically uninterested or disaffected, the 29th annual survey of Who's Who Among American High School Students (1998) offers some sobering statistics about our nation's highest achievers: 53 percent indicated that cheating is "no big deal," and more than 80 percent admit to some form of academic dishonesty. Somewhat ironically, 46 percent indicated that a decline in social and moral values was the biggest problem facing their generation.

The Changing Pressures of College

Cheating among our nation's best and brightest students highlights a second but related value shift over the past several decades. As market values were replacing social values and inequalities in wealth were widening from Main Street to Wall Street, higher education—and students' pursuit of it—was undergoing profound changes of its own. Perhaps first and most important among these changes was the reason why students were pursuing college degrees. The most comprehensive barometer of these shifts comes from the 40-plus-year-old Cooperative Institutional Resource Program conducted by Alexander Astin and his colleagues at UCLA. Astin et al.'s (1997) research indicates that the vast majority of today's students entering college are oriented toward becoming "very well off financially" (approximately 80 percent say this is a "very important" or "essential" goal) while only a minority, approximately 35 percent, seek to "develop a meaningful philosophy of life." This pattern represents the opposite of the goals of entering first-year college students in the late 1960s, when the majority regarded higher education as a journey of personal, intellectual, and moral growth, and not merely a means to social status and material wealth.

This commodification of education was accompanied by two additional forces that, taken together, most certainly fueled the rising epidemic of cheating: grade inflation and increasing competition. Specifically, the average grade point average (GPA) among college undergraduates rose from approximately 2.5 in 1960 to 3.0 in 2000. Moreover, while average GPAs at private and public colleges differed very little in 1960 (less than one-tenth of a point higher at private institutions), the gap had widened to nearly four-tenths of a point by 2000 (Rojstaczer 2009). The reasons behind these differences in change over time are not clear. It is clear, however, that these increases in GPA have been accompanied by a corresponding increase in competition for admissions into our nation's colleges and universities, particularly among high-achieving students (Bound, Hershbein, and Long 2009).

Finally, in addition to the shift in cultural values over the past few decades that have made cheating more acceptable and prevalent, the emergence and almost universal availability of digital technologies (from the Internet to cell phones) have made cheating quicker and easier. For example, while would-be plagiarists once had to retype every word from the printed sources they wished to pilfer, the Internet and cut-and-paste technology have made it possible to swipe large swaths of another person's writing in a matter of seconds. Similarly, handwritten "cheat sheets" are fast being replaced with covert notes stored in digital devices such as calculators and cell phones. This is not to say that these technological innovations have *caused* an increase in academic dishonesty (for a discussion of this conjecture, see McCabe and Stephens 2006), but they have made it faster and simpler.

Keyed In

All the exterior doors at Chapel Hill High School (Chapel Hill, North Carolina) have recently been rekeyed after administrators discovered that students had obtained and copied a school master key to gain access to teachers' offices (Hartness 2008).

Over the past several years, students have had access to and copied tests and answer keys and distributed them among fellow students. Students passed around duplicates of the tests and answers, and even shared them by cell phones.

The entire adult school community was in great shock after this situation came to light. Apparently, the key was passed down each year as classes graduated. Clearly, many students knew what was going on but never said anything. Consequences were given to some students as the scheme was uncovered, but administrators and teachers are focusing now on finding ways to prevent this from happening again.

What Happens When Values Shift

There is little doubt that the growth of academic cheating over the past four decades can be attributed to these broader cultural shifts—toward market values and materialism, away from personal meaning and moral integrity; toward inflated grades and increased competition, away from authentic learning and valid assessments of that learning. Cheating, after all, is a viable strategy for students who are primarily interested in the extrinsic goals or rewards (e.g., grades, degrees, money, status, etc.) associated with academic success. Conversely, cheating makes little sense for students who are primarily interested in developing their understanding or mastering new skills. As noted earlier, many students believe that cheating is wrong but make a conscious choice to do it anyway in order to meet the pressures to keep up or get ahead.

Here's how one student, who believes cheating is morally wrong, explains the conflict and her decision to cheat:

I think that cheating is morally wrong, but when you are under the pressure of trying to maintain good grades it is hard not to give into the temptation because these grades determine what kind of college you attend and what kind of job you receive.

For this student and many others today, getting an A is more important than morality. Their intrinsic understanding and acknowledgment that cheating is wrong is trumped by their pursuit of As and the extrinsic rewards associated with academic "success" (Pope 2001). This value orientation or ordering, and the widespread problem of academic cheating associated with it, is not simply a product of "bad" students who don't know right from wrong. There are broader social and cultural forces at play that affect the behavior of both adolescents and adults in our society. From the real-life trials of Martha Stewart, Ken Lay, and Bernie Madoff to the televised tribulations of popular reality shows such as *The Apprentice*, we live in a culture where lying, stealing, and deceiving have become the commonplace means that our icons of success use to advance their personal wealth and power. The message to our children and adolescents seems clear: material success comes before moral integrity; doing well is more important than doing good.

As Callahan's (2004) work makes clear (and daily news releases remind us), cheating is not a problem that is confined to nor created by adolescents. It is a complex sociological and psychological problem that seems to pervade nearly every aspect of our society. With this in mind, academic cheating among students at all levels is best understood as a reflection of our nation's cultural values and adult behavior. Accordingly, schools alone cannot remedy the problem. They can and must, however, actively promote better values and behaviors.

Changing School Culture to Promote Academic Integrity: A Conceptual Model

To change individuals we must change culture; to change culture we must change individuals. Thus, a comprehensive effort to promote academic integrity must not only focus on changing students, it must also include more systemic, cultural change. This toolkit has been designed to do both, offering a broad range of approaches to changing school culture and individual behavior in a dynamic, mutually reinforcing fashion.

As we have indicated, in the fall of 2007 we began the *Achieving with Integrity* project to promote academic integrity in a diverse set of public high schools.[4] The model we created to guide our efforts was rooted in both theory and research that have long proved effective at the postsecondary level. We know, for example, that academic dishonesty is reduced by a third to a half in schools that have created a culture of academic integrity (e.g., McCabe and Trevino 1993). School communities create a culture of academic integrity through the use and integration of multiple approaches (there is no single silver bullet). As depicted in Figure 1.1, our model (and the one that serves to guide the organization of this toolkit) consists of four dimensions that, when operating together, create a culture where "achieving with integrity" becomes the norm.

At the top of the model, and infusing all other components, are the *Core Values* of respect, trust, honesty, responsibility, effort, and learning (cf. Center for Academic Integrity 1999). Values are ideas or concepts that we hold close and use to guide us, particularly in times of crisis or uncertainty. They serve as both foundation and guideposts. As such, *core values* should be clearly communicated and widely embraced within the school community (McCabe and Trevino 1993). Core values also establish the moral link that can be made to the behaviors associated with academic integrity.

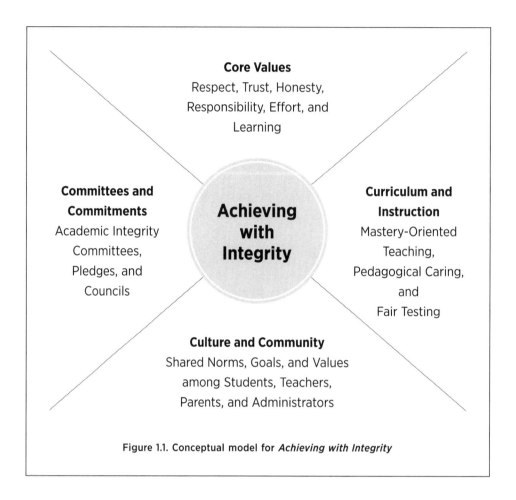

Figure 1.1. Conceptual model for *Achieving with Integrity*

Moving counterclockwise, the next component is *Committees and Commitments*. These include, but are not limited to, the creation of Academic Integrity Committees (as we call them) that serve as oversight and catalyzing bodies. Chapter 2 offers detailed suggestions for creating such committees, and chapter 3 and 4 the kind of commitments (e.g., honor codes) and councils Academic Integrity Committees might help to create. It is important to emphasize that any of these strategies will only be effective if there is authentic community buy-in to create a culture that values academic integrity, particularly among students.

Accordingly, the third component of this model, *Culture and Community*, emphasizes the importance of developing strategies to engage and sustain the support not only of teacher and students but also of administrators and parents. One simple commitment that the school community can make to the Academic Integrity Committee (AIC) is to provide it a budget to support AIC projects, publications, and representative participation in relevant conferences or professional development. Section III of this toolkit offers a range of suggestions for student-led projects and initiatives that promote a culture of integrity (chapter 5) as well as ways in which parents and other partners might be encouraged to participate and contribute (chapter 6).

The fourth and final component of this model, *Curriculum and Instruction*, focuses more squarely on what is taught and how it is taught. Some of the most effective strategies in support of academic integrity can take place as teachers make relevant pedagogical and curricular connections and students continue to advocate for academic integrity through their own initiatives. In section IV (chapters 7 and 8), there are a variety of recommendations and strategies offered to teachers such as integrating the theme of integrity into their class expectations, syllabi, discussions, and procedures.

Distressed Parent Letter

Dear Dr. Wangaard,

I am a distressed parent of a 9th and 4th grader at a prestigiously academic school here in South Florida. My 9th grader will be graduating in three weeks in a very beautiful and honoring ceremony. She has plugged and toiled to graduate with high honors since the school academic standards are very high.

I was deeply saddened to learn that seven of her classmates were caught cheating on an exam last week, and became more distressed to learn that this was not the first time. I am the last to cast a stone but the headmaster does not want to carry out the school handbook's . . . discipline which is a suspension because it will affect their heading off to the elite Northeast boarding schools they have been accepted to. He has decided to give them a zero on the exam, LET them RETAKE it and give them a low effort and consideration for others grade on this last quarter report card.

I feel that they should be suspended and not be honored with graduating and receiving academic awards with those who earned it honestly (such as my daughter). My husband and I are passionate about teaching ethics to our children. We feel our young son will get the wrong message and see that it is okay to cheat at this school. We have applied to send him to a different school and are anxiously waiting for a space to open up. It might not this summer and we don't want him to return with a scarlet letter because his parents rocked the boat.

In one way I see how these kids have been driven to it. I know their parents and instead of do your best, do it well and do it honestly, the message is get ahead at all costs. As the minority what should we do?

I anxiously wait to hear from you.

Most sincerely,
[Name omitted]

It's Time to Take Action

At this time, the topic of academic integrity appears to be a low priority in many of our public high schools. We hope the concerns raised in this book can engage administrators and teachers alike to focus time and energy to address the issues associated with academic integrity in their school. This toolkit is provided for educators to help them organize an AIC to begin a set of processes, such as identifying core values that support academic integrity, creating a strategic plan to advance a culture of integrity, and conducting climate surveys and dialogues that include students and teachers, to assess and discuss the adequacy of their school's current integrity policies and procedures.

The epidemic of cheating has festered too long. It's time for school leaders to undertake efforts to address the problem. We believe this problem can be turned into an opportunity not only to promote the value and importance of academic integrity but also to advance the development of a school culture that affirms personal ethical/moral commitment and action. To miss or avoid this opportunity is to deny a core mission of public education to support the development of an ethical citizenry in moral learning communities. We welcome all our colleagues in secondary education to join in the mission and implement the strategies in this toolkit to support academic integrity.

NOTES

1. Our survey instructions, as well as those of McCabe, ask students to confine their responses to the current academic year (e.g., "During this school year, how often have you . . . ?"). Using this approach, approximately 80 percent of students report cheating on homework; 60 percent, cheating on a test; and 50 percent, plagiarizing materials. Summing across all behaviors yields the 90 percent figure.

2. Major funding for this three-year (2007–10) intervention project was provided by the John Templeton Foundation, the Richard Davoud Donchian Foundation, and Wright Investors' Service. The ideas and opinions expressed in this toolkit are those of the authors and do not necessarily reflect the views of the funders.

3. Numerous studies using cross-sectional analyses (i.e., comparing the beliefs and behaviors of students across two or more decades, such as the 1970s vs. the 1990s) have found significant increases in *self-reported* cheating behavior over time (McCabe & Bowers 1994; Schab 1991).

4. For a complete description of this project, see www.ethicsed.org/programs/integrity-works/index.htm.

COMMITMENTS
and COMMITTEES

CHAPTER 2

Establishing an Academic Integrity Committee (AIC)

I would like for our school to let everyone know how important integrity is. How it can help you in the world beyond high school. How it can help you become respected and successful.

High school student

An effective team is required for any meaningful change initiative in a school. The main strategy proposed in this toolkit is the organization and administration of an Academic Integrity Committee (AIC) as a team approach to promote integrity. AIC founders should have the backing of the school, and district administration should recognize the need for a long-term commitment to the AIC's mission. Organizers should also strategically recruit influential leaders of the school community to include administration, faculty, and students, as well as parents and other interested community members. The mission to promote integrity will require the synergy and commitment of this diverse group.

Each AIC in our project approached its organizational structure in a slightly different way. All the schools initially had clear administration support. One AIC was at first led by a teacher, another by an academic department head, and a third by a school counselor. In year two, an assistant principal took over the leadership of one team. In addition, in one school a very active parent volunteer core evolved. One school's administration was required to pay a stipend to its AIC sponsor, while the other leaders were all in voluntary positions. Student participation also varied among the schools, with the most active student membership leading to a greater number of completed projects.

The leader of an AIC should have excellent team-building and committee facilitation skills or be willing to develop these skills. Team building and effective meeting facilitation are vital in beginning any new volunteer team. An AIC leader should also recognize and be willing to face the difficulties and opposition that are almost guaranteed parts of the upcoming process. Opposition from faculty, individual administrators, parents, and students has been observed in the modest sample of four schools. The greatest challenge, however, is time, and the urgency of other school priorities.

This chapter will provide an outline of activities, worksheets, and forms to recruit AIC members, define the AIC mission, draft a strategic plan, and provide suggestions for how to begin communicating that plan to the school community.

Whose Honor Code?

A colleague who was sponsoring an Academic Integrity Committee shared the following dilemma:

> We are trying to spread the Academic Honor Code (AHC) and promote awareness too, but we have public relations issue[s] when discipline goes awry. One of my colleagues recently spoke to me about his disappointment about the administration (when confronted by a parent) not respecting the consequences he had proposed with regard to an alleged violation of academic integrity.
>
> My colleague felt that the AHC was a sham and that we are hypocrites to promote it when (in his view) the administration doesn't enforce punishments for offenders. My first reaction was to say that it would be unfortunate and excessive to tar the AHC—or disavow it—even if a given case doesn't work out as one or more of us might like, but also that we need to address this openly and honestly even if it proves to be embarrassing. As I said when interviewed for a newspaper: we are a work in progress.
>
> How would you advise me to proceed? I'm trying to plan ahead, to help manage a potential situation before it gets out of control. I'm respecting my colleague's request that I not get involved, for now, but I'm concerned that this may become a public event that will cast aspersion[s] on something for which we're trying—as you are—to get good press.

AIC Invitation Letter

Effective recruitment of AIC members can be facilitated by clear communication. Personal invitations are most effective when attempting to start a committee. An invitation letter can help inform potential members of the mission, time requirements, and duration of your request. A sample letter is provided on the CD-ROM in the back of this book. You may print this on existing letterhead or use it to write a more personal message of your own.

COMMITTEE RECRUITMENT

An Academic Integrity Committee (AIC) is the essential implementation committee for schools to advance a culture of integrity. Working in collaboration with the school administration, the AIC should represent the diversity of the school community, and it can be responsible for a variety of tasks. Use this worksheet to identify and prioritize membership for a 10- to 14-member AIC.

Potential AIC Members

Prioritize (1 = Very important, 2 = Important, 3 = Helpful) recruitment of AIC members

Administration	Faculty	Staff	Students
Coaches	Parents	Community members	Other

Use the scale above to prioritize the groups you'd like to recruit. Then use the chart below to determine how many people to recruit from each group. Assign the responsibility of recruitment to committed individuals who will contact potential members personally. AIC founders are encouraged to recruit influential student leaders.

Member Group	Target Number	Who Will Recruit?
Administration		
Faculty		
Students		
Parents		

Committee Recruitment

Successful formation of a diverse AIC requires good planning and proactive recruitment. A draft mission/objective statement should be created to inform potential members of the committee's goals. Draft a mission statement that you will use to recruit members to the AIC.

Example: *The Academic Integrity Committee's (AIC) mission is to promote a learning environment at [school name here] that honors and supports the principles of honest effort and achievement in all the academic and extracurricular activities. The AIC will support the understanding and commitment to academic integrity and implementation of integrity policies.*

Draft mission statement:

Committee Introductory Meeting

There are a few simple guidelines for hosting a positive committee meeting that will encourage people to participate during the meeting, work on committee tasks between meetings, and remain engaged in the process. A number of suggestions are noted here:

Meeting Guidelines

1. Establish clear objectives for each meeting.
2. Create an agenda to meet your objectives and distribute the agenda before the meeting.
3. Start and end meetings on time and don't exceed 90 minutes.
4. Remember to include *people* in the meeting process by taking time to practice team-building strategies (through mixers, use of names, and small-group assignments during and in between meetings), and always have refreshments!
5. Establish group norms of respect and agree upon statements to help stay on topic such as, "That's a great idea, but for right now let's focus on this agenda item."
6. Use communication tools effectively (flip charts, SMART Boards, Power-Point projectors, minutes).
7. Summarize agreements, next steps, and assignments at the end of each meeting.

Suggested First Meeting Agenda

I. Welcome
   A. Introductions with brief mixer
   B. Review of need (provide essays for follow-up reading)
   C. Meeting logistics (breaks, end, restrooms, phone use, etc.)

II. Clarification of Objectives
   A. Review and discuss mission (subcommittee follow-up)
   B. Review and discuss definition of academic integrity (subcommittee to follow-up)
   C. Begin SWOT analysis (maybe forward to second meeting)—SWOT is defined by strengths, weaknesses, opportunities, and threats that the district/school might face as it works to promote academic integrity (subcommittee to follow-up)

III. Closure
   A. Summarize agreements from meeting
   B. Affirm time and location of next meeting

AIC First Meeting Support Notes

I. Welcome
   A. Introductions
      1. Use name tags or name tents at your meeting table.
      2. Use a brief mixer activity to allow committee members a chance to learn each other's names and some basic background details. Example: at each seat, the board member will find a blank sheet of paper and a pencil or marker. Board members are asked to sketch something that is important to them in less than three minutes and be prepared to describe their sketch. After three minutes, take volunteers to start and provide participants one minute (or less) to share their names, where they work (or what grade in school), and a brief summary that explains their sketch. You will have a lot of stick figure drawings and should have some laughter to start the meeting.
      3. Obtain permission to record names and contact information to share as a committee communication list.
   B. Review of Need for AIC
      1. Provide a short relevant essay for committee members prior to meeting.
      2. Highlight research from literature:
         • 80–95 percent of students engaged in academic dishonesty
         • Pressure on students to cheat (see pages 4–7)
         • Reasons to promote academic integrity (see pages 2, 10)

II. Clarification of Objectives
   A. Allocate sufficient time to seek a consensus on the direction of your mission and agreement or clarification needed with draft. Establish a subcommittee to review the draft and meeting suggestions for revision and have subcommittee present suggested changes at next meeting
   B Invite committee to work together or in smaller groups to help define academic integrity. Have subcommittee follow-up with suggestions for revisions.
   C. SWOT Analysis. (See the following example. This activity may need to begin in meeting two.)

Strengths	Weaknesses
Volunteers on committee, great students and teachers, supportive parent community	Time, focus on issue, achievement pressure, rationalizations (cheating doesn't hurt anyone, etc.)

Opportunities	Threats
Student leadership interest, clearly define cheating, improve focus on authentic learning, grant availability	Other school priorities, student peer pressure, achievement pressure, faculty resistance to perception of added responsibilities

Sketch the SWOT analysis box on flip chart paper, or use the handout on pages 22–24 and the enclosed CD-ROM. Have committee members begin the process of brainstorming district/school strengths, weaknesses, opportunities, and threats to your stated mission to promote academic integrity. Depending on the amount of time available, assign a subcommittee to follow up and finish the analysis for the next committee meeting.

Academic Integrity Committee (AIC) Meeting Outline Suggested Template

I. Attendance
- Committee members should sign in on the attendance sheet and keep contact information current.
- At each meeting, note the expectation of "present or accounted for" where AIC members should inform chairperson if they cannot attend a meeting.
- Recognize the expectation that members should formally resign from the AIC if regular attendance is not possible.
- Recognize the expectation that members should be engaged with some subcommittee assignment.
- Encourage the expectation that members should attend meetings with their AIC notebook. An AIC notebook is recommended to include (1) contact information for AIC members, (2) a section for meeting notes, (3) a section for AIC policies, (4) a section for AIC bibliography or relevant essays, and (5) a section for ongoing project notes.

II. Welcome
- Plan some short greeting or team-building exercise to welcome all members.
- Introduce new members or guests.

III. Review Notes
- Distribute and review notes from the last meeting.
- Seek clarifications and agreement regarding what was done and what was assigned.
  - These notes should have been electronically distributed soon after the last meeting.
  - Printed notes should be three-hole punched for placement in the AIC notebook.

IV. Review Agenda
- Distribute printed agendas to all committee members.
- Seek committee agreement on the current agenda (reprioritize if necessary).
- Add any new items members might want to address (new items that do not need immediate attention should be put on the agenda for the next meeting).
- Chairperson should suggest a timeline (stay flexible but focused) for each item to help complete a reasonable agenda for each meeting.
- Recognize during the meeting when agenda item(s) need to be moved to a future meeting.
- Seek to include one AIC training/teaching activity during each meeting regarding the topic of integrity. Examples: sharing practices from other schools, a relevant story or current event, academic integrity research.

V. Executing the Agenda
- Take one topic/item at a time.
- Stay focused on the topic.
- Defer detail work to a subcommittee.
  - Subcommittees can draft, write, and edit better than full committees.
  - Subcommittees can research and prepare detailed suggestions for committee review.
- Identify subcommittee members and clear tasks for follow-up.
- Set dates for follow-up and record them in the meeting notes.
- Identify the next implementation steps before moving on to the next item.

VI. Meeting Closure
- Review agreements and follow-up assignments.
- Celebrate progress.
- Open reflection on ways to improve.
- Set a new meeting date. (Attempt to keep the same schedule each month—for example, the first Thursday.)

Thank members for their participation.

Academic Integrity Committee (AIC) Meeting Notes (Sample)

Note: The following is an example of a filled-in page of meeting notes. There is a blank template on the CD-ROM in the back of this book.

AIC MEETING NOTES

Date: _____

Meeting # _____   Meeting location: _____

Attendance summary #: _____   _____Admin _____Faculty _____Students _____Parents

Meeting start _____:_____   Meeting end _____:_____

Agenda and meeting notes:

1.

2.

3.

4.

Next meeting date/time: _____

Task follow-up:

Task Description	Members Assigned	Next Steps	Timeline
Example: Complete the AIC mission statement	Mission Statement Subcommittee (2–3 people)	Edit draft AIC mission statement with comments from meeting Forward edited draft to committee members one week before next meeting Compile any follow-up suggestions that result from editing for next meeting	Return to next meeting with edited draft of mission statement and any suggestions for revision
Example: Revise definition of academic integrity		Using comments from last meeting, edit definition of academic integrity	Present edited definition of academic integrity for committee approval
Example: Compile SWOT analysis		Compile notes from SWOT analysis and identify any themes for each topic and themes that cross topics for presentation at next meeting	Compilation and presentation prepared for next meeting

WORKING MISSION STATEMENT

AIC's draft mission statement:

Subcommittee's revised language:

AIC-approved mission statement:

Date: _____

DEFINING ACADEMIC INTEGRITY

Directions: As a full committee, or in smaller groups, review, edit, and/or revise the following definition of academic integrity from the honor policies of Langley High School in McLean, Virginia. Record your discussion points and write out your revised definition.

Academic Integrity can be defined by honest academic work in which (1) the ideas and the writing of others are properly cited; (2) students submit their own work for tests and assignments without unauthorized assistance; (3) students do not provide unauthorized assistance to others; and (4) students report their research or accomplishments accurately.

Discussion points:

Revised definition:

If more than one team revised a definition, compare your drafts.

Final working definition of academic integrity:

SWOT ANALYSIS

A SWOT analysis is a method to identify all the strengths, weaknesses, opportunities, and threats that the AIC faces in creating an academic integrity initiative at your school.

Strengths	Weaknesses

Opportunities	Threats

SWOT ANALYSIS SUMMARY FORM

As a subcommittee assignment or with the full committee, summarize your SWOT analysis (start on flip chart paper) and prioritize each strength, weakness, opportunity, or threat with a number: 1 = High priority, 2 = Medium priority, and 3 = Low priority. For each item that has been assigned a 1 or 2 priority label, identify potential follow-up ideas. Selecting high-priority items first, assign committee members to create strategic steps to implement follow-up ideas (see planning form). Refer to Table 2.1 on page 28 and the Implementation Model to Support Academic Integrity in Schools (Figure 2.1) for potential AIC activities. When time is available, complete the same step with medium-priority items.

Strengths	Priority	Follow-up Idea	Assigned
Weaknesses	**Priority**	**Follow-up Idea**	**Assigned**

(continued on next page)

Opportunities	Priority	Follow-up Idea	Assigned

Threats	Priority	Follow-up Idea	Assigned

STRATEGIC PLANNING FORM

Date: _____

After a SWOT analysis, use this form to create follow-up steps for one idea. Discuss this idea as a committee, prioritize it with other ideas and assign a time to implement. Save this form in a strategic planning file.

Committee members: _____

_____

SWOT analysis item and follow-up idea: _____

_____

Specific objective/goal: _____

_____

Follow-up Steps (Be as detailed as possible)	Time Frame	Due Date

Suggested Outline for Meeting Two

I.   Welcome
  A. Introductions with brief mixer (share a positive event from the past month)
  B. Review of minutes from last meeting
  C. Consensus agreement on current meeting agenda

II. Continuing Business
  A. Subcommittee presentation to review, discuss, affirm (if possible) AI Committee mission statement
    1. Discussion/editing
    2. Approval
  B. Subcommittee presentation of definition of academic integrity
    1. Discussion/editing
    2. Approval
  C. Subcommittee presentation on completed SWOT analysis (strengths, weaknesses, opportunities, threats) of district/school as it relates to academic integrity
    1. Full committee discuss strategies to build on strengths and connect to opportunities (see ideas in Table 2.1)
    2. Full committee discuss strategies to address weakness and resist threats (see ideas in Table 2.1)

III. New Business
  A. In light of SWOT analysis and using the following planning form, brainstorm short-term AIC goals (subcommittee to follow up)

IV. Closure
  A. Summarize agreements from the meeting.
  B. Summarize individuals assigned to next steps.
  C. Affirm the time and location of the next meeting.

Implementation Model to Support Academic Integrity in Schools

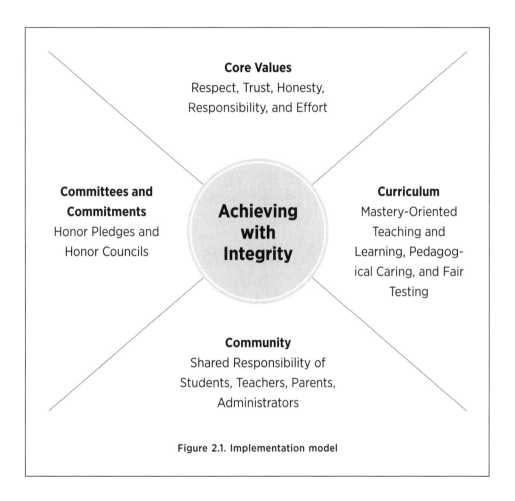

Figure 2.1. Implementation model

This implementation model offers a systematic approach to promote academic integrity in high schools. Supported by research, this model outlines goals for school communities to organize a diverse Academic Integrity Committee (AIC) to identify core values in support of commitments to academic integrity, which would affect the culture and curriculum of the school. Table 2.1 offers suggested activities that an AIC might include within their strategic plan.

Table 2.1.
Suggested Academic Integrity Committee (AIC) activities

Community	Core Values	Commitments	Curriculum
Organize an AIC to include students, faculty, administration, and parents	Clarify and articulate connection between school's core values and academic integrity	Sustain an AIC with a written mission, code of conduct, and monthly meetings	Create AIC information brochures, flyers, posters, cards, other handouts, videos for school TV network
Recruit student AIC members to support AIC activities. Recruit adult AIC members with representatives from relevant disciplines	Review and seek administration and board support to define the school's mission to include academic integrity as a core value	Research, write, and implement a multiple-year AIC strategic plan	Develop faculty professional development activities to support teacher recognition of classroom procedures and instructional strategies to advance academic integrity
Recruit incoming first-year students to AIC with introduction to high school integrity standards in first-year orientation	Clearly connect school integrity policies to school's core values in variety of school media	Review, revise, and gain approval to publish clear policies, procedures, and rules for teachers to implement in support of academic integrity	Create AIC lessons to integrate into relevant subject areas
Maintain current AIC information about mission, projects, and recruitment on link from school website	Connect school's core values to enforcement of integrity policies	Obtain administration and school board support to reinforce academic integrity policies	Publish relevant academic integrity policies, procedures, and rules in student handbook, school website, and class syllabi
Connect integrity messages to mentoring programs	Create activities that help students and faculty define academic integrity in light of core values	Provide positive recognition for students/faculty demonstrating academic integrity	Seek to integrate integrity themes within reading assignments
Recruit drama classes or tech (video) classes to produce AIC skits/videos	Create messages to refute any subculture reinforcing nonacademic performance, where students are not fully engaged in school	Organize an honor court to adjudicate integrity violations	Administer surveys to promote student body engagement in integrity topics

(continued on next page)

(Table 2.1, continued)

Community	Core Values	Commitments	Curriculum
Encourage school and community librarians to publish clear academic integrity messages and citation procedures	Create messages to refute high-performing students' rationalizations for academic dishonesty	Provide AIC a budget to purchase relevant resources for its mission, offer stipend to AIC chair, and maintain membership in professional associations	Create an AIC information video or skits and show/perform at school lunches, assemblies, school TV network
Engage parents through activities offered at parent associations and orientation meetings	Find and publish within community positive stories related to academic integrity and the connection to core values	Integrate integrity themes into faculty professional development goal statements	Write articles for school newspaper or principal's newsletters and school webpage
Request that community members address integrity issues during career days or college fairs	Design and implement discussion activities that support society's need for academic integrity	Design and implement a qualitative and quantitative evaluation plan to guide the AIC's strategic plan	Promote teacher procedures to reduce cheating (e.g., teachers' explanation of expectations, use of different test forms, clear limits for group work, Turnitin.com)
Solicit local business community support for AIC budget and note support on website and publications	Recommend the hiring of teachers and administrators who will proactively support academic integrity as a core value of education	Consider an honor code and/or pledge for students to affirm	Promote student behaviors to reduce cheating—making the choice to learn, being prepared, seeking appropriate help in timely manner
AIC committee members personally recruit middle school students from middle school honor society		Seek fair and efficient enforcement of academic integrity policies	Create integrity lessons and activities for homerooms or advisory classes, new student orientations, students facing honor violation penalties
Maintain dialogue with other schools and relevant professional associations		Maintain appropriate records of integrity violations	Create and present lessons for students in middle schools
Publish stories and evaluations of school integrity program (newsletters, website, conferences, journals)			

SUGGESTED AIC EXECUTIVE COMMITTEE ROLES AND DEFINITIONS

Formal leadership roles can support your Academic Integrity Committee (AIC) identify a collaborative team and establish clear responsibilities to help your AIC be more successful. The following roles and definitions of responsibilities are suggested to include student participation. Committee roles should also include clear service dates (with opportunity to reenlist) with staggered dates of service to help the AIC maintain an experienced leadership core. As a full committee, or executive committee, rank each role for your AIC follow-up (1 = Very important, 2 = Important, 3 = Maybe helpful, and 4 = Not interested).

Executive Committee Roles and Definitions	Rank Priority to Your AIC (1–4)
Chairperson (adult) 1. Help guide AIC to establish a strategic plan and work with other AIC officers and standing subcommittees to set annual agenda to meet strategic plan 2. Work with other officers to set meeting agendas 3. Work with other board members to plan and facilitate meetings 4. Work with secretaries (adult and student) to ensure effective communication within AIC 5. Along with student leaders, represent AIC to school administration, faculty, and parent community 6. Maintain connection between AIC mission, narratives, and projects 7. Ensure some form of evaluation takes place each year	
Vice-chair or co-chair (adult) 1. Assist the chairperson in meeting all responsibilities	
Student president (junior or senior year) 1. Along with adult leaders, represent the AIC to school administration 2. Support other AIC officers in establishing and implementing the committee strategic plan 3. Seek to represent and recruit student participation on the committee 4. Encourage student engagement and leadership of committee projects 5. Participate in a minimum of one standing committee and one project committee	
Student vice president (sophomore or junior year) 1. Support other AIC officers in establishing and implementing the committee strategic plan 2. Seek to represent and recruit student participation on the committee 3. Encourage student engagement and leadership of committee projects 4. Participate in a minimum of one standing committee and one project committee	
Secretary (adult) 1. Record minutes/notes of each meeting 2. Track board member attendance 3. Work with other officers to edit and distribute meeting minutes/notes 4. Keep a record of minutes/notes with specific attention to volunteers for subcommittee assignments with task review dates 5. Report on minutes and tasks completed and remaining at each meeting 6. Keep permanent records of all AIC narratives, including mission, strategic plan, budget, meeting notes, and evaluations	

(continued on next page)

(continued)

Executive Committee Roles and Definitions	Rank Priority to Your AIC (1–4)
Student secretary 1. Collaborate with the adult secretary in recording, editing, and distributing meeting notes	
Treasurer 1. Track the AIC budget for income and expenditures 2. Serve as the lead organizer of any AIC fundraising 3. Collaborate on AIC grant writing	
Permanent Subcommittees	
Mission and narratives 1. Create and maintain AIC narratives that can include the strategic plan; mission statement; AIC code of conduct; commitment of stakeholders; definitions of academic integrity, core values supporting the mission, and cheating behaviors; AIC slogan; recommended honor policies; honor codes; honor pledges; Honor Council; and recommended teacher practices 2. Help the AIC chairperson keep projects consistent with the mission 3. Evaluate all AIC projects in light of the mission, core values, and strategic plan	
Communication 1. Communicate the AIC mission and projects to all school communities (administration, faculty, students, parents, local community, and funders) 2. Create and update AIC logo and slogan 3. Develop communication strategies that might use e-mail, phone, AIC blog or website, publications, school announcements, and school publications (handbooks, policy books, student papers, posters) 4. Use AIC narratives to create and publish press releases, brochures, and communications with parents 5. Work with administration to include integrity themes in faculty professional development, student orientations, etc. 6. Collaborate on AIC grant writing	
Technology 1. Support the AIC in the access and use of technology to support the communication of projects and activities through a website or blog 2. Create links with AIC subcommittees to have support from other members of the school community, such as videography, printing, computer design and publishing, and Internet and web services	
Evaluation 1. Ensure an annual evaluation component is included in the AIC strategic plan 2. Work to implement the evaluation plan with suggestion to alternate years of assessment of student and faculty attitudes, opinions, and behaviors as related to integrity themes	

AIC SUGGESTIONS FOR SUCCESS

There are many practices that can help AICs become successful. The following suggestions are provided to help structure and administer an AIC. As a full committee, or in executive committee, prioritize each suggestion for your AIC follow-up (1 = Very important, 2 = Important, 3 = Maybe helpful, and 4 = Not interested).

Suggestion	Rank Priority to Your AIC (1–4)
Leadership	
Establish an AIC leadership team (including students) to include a chairperson, vice-chairperson, and secretary	
Recruit participants who represent the diversity of the school community (faculty from various school departments, ages, and interests of students, administration, and parents)	
Clearly communicate that AIC membership requires participants to contribute a minimum of one to two hours of postmeeting follow-up each month	
Meetings	
Seek to establish a regular meeting date (for example, the first Thursday of the month)	
Prepare a premeeting agenda developed with attention to results and the next steps identified at the previous meeting	
Time the meeting agenda and respectfully hold to that agenda unless the committee agrees to diverge from the planned timing	
Include some brief greeting/team-building focus at the start of each meeting	
Record attendance and establish a "present or accounted for" expectation for all meetings—if you can't show up, you inform the chairperson in advance or explain why you could not attend ASAP after the meeting time	
Record meeting notes, transmit the notes back to members ASAP after the meeting, and focus on the next tasks to be completed	
Exchange two communications between each AIC meeting: 1. Notes that highlight the next steps and next meeting date soon after the meeting's conclusion, and 2. A reminder of tasks to be completed 7 to 10 days before the next meeting	
Action steps	
Create a clear AIC mission statement and conduct standards: • Expectation that members demonstrate integrity and steps to follow if a violation occurs • Attendance expectation and formal resignation request if leaving AIC • Confidentiality requirements • Expectation for task follow-up	
Inform AIC members of effective research-based practices in support of academic integrity	
Create an AIC library of resources	
Write an AIC strategic plan to prioritize activities (with a two- to three-year vision)	
Reflect regularly that AIC activities are designed to advance the stated mission	

AIC CODE OF CONDUCT

Creating a code of conduct can be a useful exercise for the Academic Integrity Committee to translate its mission into practical norms of behavior. Some AICs discuss and/or revise their code of conduct annually and then have their committee members sign their code of conduct each year.

Sample Code of Conduct

The Academic Integrity Committee (AIC) Code of Conduct

As a member of the AIC, I will:

- Commit to attending as many meetings as possible.
- Notify the committee chair if I cannot attend a meeting.
- Fully participate in each meeting and complete follow-up assignments.
- Protect the confidentiality of committee discussions and avoid using names of individuals in cases I might present.
- Encourage student voice and participation.
- Learn about and demonstrate the practices of academic integrity.
- Actively promote and support the implementation of academic integrity policies within the school community.
- Inform the AIC's executive committee of my own violations of this code and support the committee's disciplinary actions.

Draft local code of conduct:

Subcommittee's revised language:

AIC-approved code of conduct:

Date: _____

The sample code of conduct was provided by the West Haven High School Academic Integrity Committee, West Haven, CT, 2008.

DEFINING AIC VOCABULARY

Academic Integrity Committee Activity: Use this worksheet for your AIC and/or use a flip chart (or SMART Board); designate someone to record notes. Lead the AIC in a discussion on definitions for the following terms, or terms you believe the school community should define as they relate to academic integrity. Discuss whether the AIC recognizes other terms or vocabulary that should be part of its awareness campaign. Compare your consensus definitions to formal published definitions. Publish your consensus definitions for your school in the student handbook, posters, online, or in the student newspaper.

Vocabulary	Published Definitions	Consensus Definition
Cheat	To practice fraud or trickery; to violate rules dishonestly	
Crib sheet	A sheet containing information (as test answers) used secretly for cheating; a written or graphic aid (as a sheet of notes) that can be referred to for help in understanding or remembering something complex	
Fabricate	To make up for the purpose of deception	
Honest	Free from fraud or deception: legitimate, truthful; genuine, real	
Integrity	Firm adherence to a code of especially moral or artistic values: incorruptibility; an unimpaired condition: soundness; the quality or state of being complete or undivided: completeness	
Paraphrasing	A restatement of a text, passage, or work giving the meaning in another form	
Plagiarize	To steal and pass off (the ideas or words of another) as one's own: use (another's production) without crediting the source; to commit literary theft: present as new and original an idea or product derived from an existing source	
Reference/ citation	Something (as a sign or indication) that refers a reader or consulter to another source of information (as a book or passage)	

These definitions can be found at Merriam-Webster Online, www.m-w.com.

NEUTRALIZER WORKSHEET

Academic Integrity Committee Activity: Neutralizers are arguments or excuses people create to rationalize their cheating behavior. A helpful strategy to promote academic integrity is to expose the typical excuses and help students take responsibility for their own behaviors. Working in groups of two or three, brainstorm strategies for the AIC to resist the logic of "the neutralizers" and then identify who should implement the idea and when. Review the example for "Denial of moral issue."

Student Neutralizer	Ideas to Resist Neutralizer	Who Should Implement
Denial of moral issue: "This isn't really cheating."	Examples: Cheating behaviors are defined in the student handbook, regularly described in other school media such as the student paper, assemblies, school forums, and by teachers in class Some cheating is equivalent to theft. Is that not a moral issue? Some cheating acts violate trust	The Academic Integrity Committee (AIC) helps create definitions that are published in the student handbook; school administration and AIC disseminate definitions through a variety of media and forums Attempt to revise the handbook before the next printing (May), add definitions to the school website (January), include AIC interview in the school paper (February), include introduction to AI during first-year orientation (June)
Denial of victimization: "No one is hurt."	Questions to ask: Is anyone hurt by someone cheating to gain advanced class rank, GPA, or scholarship qualification? Is anyone hurt by cheaters not mastering their subject and then becoming certified to work in their field? Is anyone hurt when cheating behaviors expand beyond homework and extend into taxes, relationships, etc.?	

(continued on next page)

(continued)

Student Neutralizer	Ideas to Resist Neutralizer	Who Should Implement
Denial of responsibility: "This was beyond my control." (Peer pressure, dead-lines, too much work, parents demand I earn an A, etc.)	Questions to ask: Who is ultimately responsible for your behavior choices? To whom are you giving that power? What other choices contributed to the pressure? What are your priorities? What other options did you have? (When?)	
Condemning the condemners: "This is a bad teacher." (Unfair, not relevant, poor instruction, terrible test)	Questions to ask: Does your finding fault with others really justify your choice to compromise a moral position? What other options did you have (and when) to help you avoid cheating?	
Higher loyalties: "I needed an A to help me get into college or earn a scholar-ship," or "I can't ignore my friend's request for help."	Questions to ask: Should our ethical standards be put aside for important goals? Does a real friend help or ask someone to violate an ethical rule? What are the consequences if you are caught?	
Other		

Online Tools

Website for Integrity

Some AICs have effectively established websites to promote their mission and provide an updated link of information to AIC members and project supporters. As of this writing, Google offers free website hosting where you can easily create and develop your site (www.sites.google.com). All your information is collected in one place, and you can control and edit who sees your pages. An alternative to setting up your own site on Google is to gain permission and support to have your school host and include your site on the school webpage. The advantage is to be completely linked to your school; however, you may lose some flexibility of when and how quickly your site is edited and updated.

Some of the suggested pages for your website include the following:

- **Home page:** the main page that lists the name of the website and any important information that viewers should see as soon as they visit your site. This can include descriptions, pictures, logos, or upcoming events.
- **Mission statement:** a phrase to describe your AIC's goals or values.
- **Staff:** a list of the members of the AIC with e-mail addresses or phone numbers.
- **Notes:** a place to write quick memos to visitors.
- **Calendar:** a section of the website where you can post meeting dates, times, and locations.
- **News or announcements:** a place where visitors can find important information, such as meeting changes or new achievements.
- **Blog:** a link to the AIC's blog.
- **Photo gallery:** pictures from AIC meetings or projects
- **Contact information:** so visitors can easily get in touch with you if they have questions or comments.

Creating an AIC Blog

An additional online tool for an AIC can be a blog. It can be linked to the "blog" page on your AIC website so that viewers have easy access. Blogger is a website that allows you to create free, easy blogs. Visit www.blogger.com to set up and start using your own blog.

Online Video

Adding a video to your Academic Integrity Committee's blog or website is an easy process. It adds exciting multimedia "pop" to your site and sometimes tells your story better than words or pictures. If you have the movie already formatted as a file on your computer, you can go to YouTube (www.youtube.com)

for instructions on how to upload your video and embed it on your website or blog. Otherwise, if your video is on a DVD, we recommend the free Leawo DVD to MP4 Converter application, which can be downloaded at www.leawo.com/dvd-to-mp4-converter.

CHAPTER 3

Systems Approach for Academic Integrity

A qualitative study of how schools describe their academic integrity programs and a review of the work of Gould and Roberts (2007); McCabe, Trevino, and Butterfield (2001a); and Bloomfield (2007) have guided us to outline a systems approach in support of academic integrity (Figure 3.1). This systems approach provides a framework for the strategic goals of an AIC. In this chapter, we intend to describe some of the narratives and policies that may result in the pursuit of the suggested systems outline. The first goal is to identify the **core values** that support an honor policy. The **honor policy** then becomes the framework for the school community's commitment to integrity. In chapter 4, we will develop in detail the organization and policies of an **Honor Council**. An Honor Council is designed to become the volunteer consultation body for the adjudication of honor violations. Chapter 5 will describe awareness activities that the students can help lead to help support a change in the school community's thinking about integrity. Chapters 7 and 8 will address **curricular strategies** and the topic of **plagiarism**, respectively.

Our project schools represented different approaches to developing the systemic model in Figure 3.1. Two AICs focused primarily on a review and revision of school policy with very little outreach into the school culture or curriculum during the project period. Two other AICs focused on creating their internal narratives, such as their AIC mission and code of conduct, and then turned to school-wide narratives, such as core value statements, honor codes, and honor pledges. With the internal narratives finalized, these two AICs developed multiple student-led projects (see chapter 5) to promote awareness and commitment to academic integrity within their school community. Simultaneously, both of these AICs also began to review and offer revised statements about their school

Students should know that work does not get easier through life and the choices they make with cheating will [have] lifetime consequences.

High school student

honor policies. At the time of this writing, one AIC has had its revisions published in the school's student handbook and the other has its policy revisions
before the school board for approval.

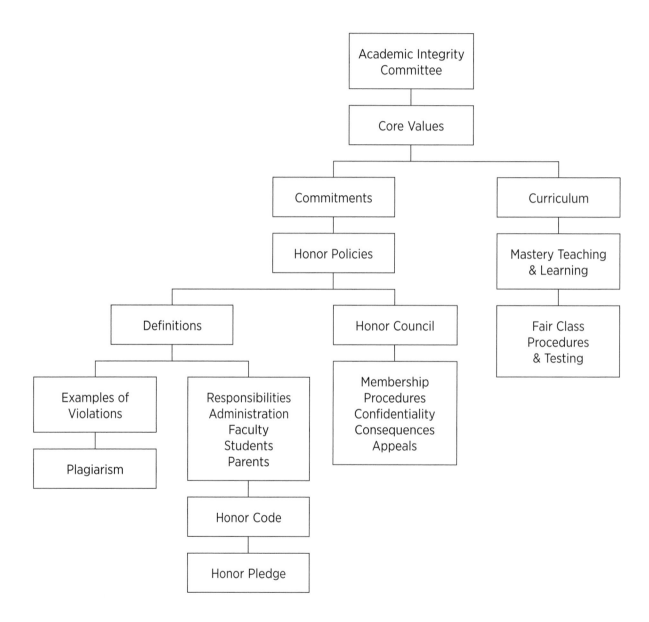

Figure 3.1. Systematic approach to developing an academic integrity initiative

Identifying Core Values

The demonstration of academic integrity can be increased when the school culture explicitly promotes core values resisting academic dishonesty (Calabrese and Cochran 1990; McCabe and Trevino 1993). The clear identification of core values such as honesty, responsibility, and fairness provides an important cognitive link to develop ethical and moral arguments that advance academic integrity.

In our own research, we find a correlation between students' reduced cheating behavior and their ability to discern and judge that cheating is a moral/ethical issue. Students have also been shown to affirm the practices of academic integrity when they understand the goal of achieving fairness and equity in grading and other assessment practices (Keith-Spiegel and Whitley 2001).

It is ultimately the responsibility of the school board and administration to articulate core values that support the school's mission. The AIC can act as an agent of the school administration to review, clarify, and advance the school's core values as they link to the principles of academic integrity.

There are a variety of ways to approach the task of linking core values to academic integrity depending on the status of the school's published mission and core values, and some of these are suggested in the following strategic steps.

The process of identifying core values can be facilitated through AIC discussion, guided class discussions that provide feedback to the AIC, and/or the solicitation of student, faculty, and community opinions via paper or electronic surveys.

The goal of this process is to establish some consensus in the school community that clearly defines core values in support of integrity. The following statement of core values is provided as an example of how an AIC can begin the process of writing an honor policy that is tied to clear ethical norms. The sample statement and strategic steps to write a core values statement is intended to help an AIC make an explicit ethical/moral link to honor policies. Our own research and others have shown that students are less likely to cheat when they make a moral/ethical link to behaviors associated with academic integrity.

Donna Andrews: A Profile in Integrity

By Bill Taylor, Oakton Community College

I turned on the television on a Saturday afternoon in 2001 and happened upon the LPGA Williams Championship. As I did, the announcer was saying that if Donna Andrews got a birdie on the eighteenth hole, she would shoot a 60. This is an incredible golf score, akin, perhaps, to hitting three home runs in one baseball game, or scoring more than 60 points in a basketball game. It happens, but very seldom, and it's a huge achievement.

Needless to say, I continued to watch. Her second shot landed on the green, but it was about 35 feet from the pin. She left the putt a couple of feet short, so she missed her 60, but she made the next putt and shot a 61—in itself an amazing score.

About fifteen minutes later the commentator announced that Donna Andrews had given herself a five on the hole instead of what seemed to be a four. As she explained it, she felt that as she followed through on her final putt she had hit the ball a second time, which is a one-stroke penalty.

One of the things about golf that makes it special among sports is that there is no referee to call penalties on the players. The players call penalties on themselves. There is a referee with each set of players, but his or her job is to explain and interpret the rules, not enforce them. In this case the referee said that he didn't think she had hit the ball a second time—perhaps she had hit the ground and only thought she had hit the ball again. The network showed the putt over and over, and you couldn't tell from watching it that she had hit the ball a second time. But Donna Andrews felt she had hit it twice so she gave herself the penalty stroke.

By doing so she was dropped into a tie with another golfer, which reduced her winnings. But that wasn't the important thing.

Clearly, her decision has something to do with integrity. At one level, it's very obvious. But as I continued to think about it, it finally occurred to me that the incident said more than just the obvious.

Donna Andrews could have said nothing about the second stroke of the ball (if indeed it actually occurred), and she could have given herself a par on the last hole and a final score of 61. And the commentators and her fellow golfers would have talked about what a wonderful round it was.

But she wouldn't have been able to enjoy her score and the acclaim of others. She wouldn't have felt good about herself if she had covered up the truth and failed to call that penalty on herself. *And if you can't enjoy it, why have it?*

B. Taylor (2004), "Donna Andrews: A Profile in Integrity." Used by permission.

Sample Statement of Core Values

Our school's mission includes the expectation of high standards in ethical behavior as well as scholarship. Academic integrity is an integral component of this mission, and we seek to foster respect (for self and others), trust in honest achievement, and positive relationships among all stakeholders in our school community. Our honor policy, honor code, and honor pledge are intended to clarify the expectations we have for all students to maintain an ethical climate that values honesty, effort, and respect for others.[1]

The core values underlying and reflected in this honor policy include the following:

- **Academic honesty,** which is demonstrated by students when the ideas and the writing of others are properly cited, when students submit their own work for tests and assignments without unauthorized assistance, when students do not provide unauthorized assistance to others, and when students report their research or accomplishments accurately.
- **Respect** for others and the learning process to demonstrate academic honesty.
- **Trust** in others to act with academic honesty as a positive community-building force in the school.
- **Responsibility** is recognized by all to demonstrate their best effort to prepare and complete academic tasks.
- **Fairness** and equity are demonstrated so that every student can experience an academic environment that is free from the injustices caused by any form of intellectual dishonesty.
- **Integrity** of all members of the school community as demonstrated by a commitment to academic honesty and support of our quest for authentic learning.

Strategic Steps

The AIC can evaluate the following steps to identify, publish, and apply core values in support of academic integrity:

1. With support/participation from the school administration, research and determine the existence of core values and academic integrity statements in school narratives (such as the mission statement as well as faculty and student handbooks).
   a. If statements exist, review them for clarity and the opportunity to use them to promote academic integrity.
   b. If statements do not exist or are unclear, determine a plan to identify core values in support of academic integrity for school community.
      i. Facilitate community dialogue (including students) to identify core values.
      ii. Administer surveys/focus groups to identify core values.
      iii. Solicit school board or school administration to draft a statement of core values.

2. Publish a statement of school core values that clearly defines each value and its connection to academic integrity.
   a. The statement of core values can be published in the faculty and student handbooks, on the school website, or on school posters.

     b.   Connect all school policies to the support of core values.

     c.   Encourage/require teachers to articulate the connection of the teaching mission to core values.

     d.   Plan and implement activities to help students recognize, discuss, and reason with core values.

3.   Assess the school community's awareness, understanding, and application of core values.

     a.   Use school climate surveys to track and measure student and faculty recognition and application of core values.

     b.   Publish the results of school climate surveys.

     c.   Review and adapt practices based on the results of school climate surveys.

The following handout may be used by an AIC or its equivalent to create a committee strategic plan to identify and publish core values in support of academic integrity.

Honor Policy

A clearly written honor policy provides a powerful narrative in the development of a school community's commitment to academic integrity. Honor policies offer an opportunity to articulate the school's core values that define the moral reason to act with integrity. Honor policies are also publications of what defines academic integrity and cheating.

A review of 93 schools that publish their honor policies revealed a variety of formats and content outlines (see Appendix II). This review also revealed that the vocabulary of honor policies can vary from school to school. In some cases honor codes were written as policy; in other cases honor codes appeared to be more appropriately defined as honor pledges. For the purpose of the following sample honor policy, we will be applying the following definitions.

Honor Policies: The purpose of an honor policy is to communicate the meaning and importance of academic integrity to the school community and to publish as policy the codes, pledges, community responsibilities, and sanctions in support of high ethical standards. Honor polices can include a number of elements:

- Affirmation of core values as they support academic integrity
- Definitions related to the implementation of an honor policy
- Responsibilities of the Academic Integrity Committee
- Responsibilities of all members of the learning community
- Honor code and honor pledge
- Role, procedures, and guidelines for an Honor Council

IDENTIFYING AND HIGHLIGHTING CORE VALUES

Use this worksheet to select tasks to help research and identify core values that can be approved by the school or district in direct support of an academic integrity initiative.

Task	Committee Members	Next Steps	Time Frame
Research school documents to identify existing core values and statements in support of integrity			
If relevant core value statements exist, create plan to integrate and publish in AIC materials (flyers, posters, policies, website, etc.)			
If relevant core value statements do not exist or are unclear, create plan with administration support to identify community consensus for core values			
Create plan to encourage administration and faculty reference to and application of core values			
Create plan to encourage student awareness, understanding, and application of core values			
Create plan to assess school community's understanding and application of core values			
Other			

Honor Code: An honor code briefly summarizes the school's honor policy, which defines the expected standards and core values of student conduct in academic affairs. The honor code can be published in the student handbook and on the school website. The purpose of an honor code is to communicate the meaning and importance of academic integrity to all members of the school community.

Honor Pledge: An honor pledge is a one- to two-sentence statement that students may write or state orally to affirm their support of the school's honor code. An honor pledge may also be written to focus singularly on a completed project or exam.

Honor Council: An Honor Council can be responsible for reviewing specific cases in which the school's honor code may have been violated. The council can make recommendations about consequences to the school administration. If students are involved on the Honor Council, the council can be an important collaboration among the students and adults to support the goal of academic integrity. The Honor Council may be organized as an extracurricular service activity for students. An Honor Council is not a court of law and acts only as a communication, review, recommendation, and education service of the school.

The sample policy presented here represents a review of 93 school websites and a synthesis of 33 high school honor policies from both public and private schools; this synthesis integrates specific policies with permission from 14 of those schools. Academic Integrity Committees are encouraged to review this policy and evaluate it for applications to their own school (Appendix II).

Sample Honor Policy

Academic integrity is defined by honest academic work where (1) the ideas and the writing of others are properly cited; (2) students submit their own work for tests and assignments without unauthorized assistance; (3) students do not provide unauthorized assistance to others; and (4) students report their research or accomplishments accurately.[2]

This policy includes the following:
- Affirmation of core values as they support academic integrity
- Definitions related to our implementation of an honor policy (see chapter 8 on plagiarism)
- Responsibilities of the Academic Integrity Committee

- Responsibilities of all members of our learning community
- Honor code and honor pledge
- Role, procedures, and guidelines for the Honor Council (see chapter 4)

Our academic mission and learning expectations call for high standards in ethical behavior as well as scholarship. Academic integrity, as defined here, is necessary to foster self-respect, achievement, and positive relationships among all stakeholders in our school community. The functions of the honor policy are to communicate the meaning and importance of academic integrity to all students of the school; to articulate and support the interest of the community in maintaining the highest standards of conduct in academic affairs; and to identify, sanction, and educate those who fail to live up to the stated expectations of the school community with regard to the following **core values**.[3]

Honesty
- Tell the truth
- Present your own work only
- Give credit for all sources

Integrity
- Act in accordance with high moral principles
- Cooperate with efforts to maintain high moral principles
- Encourage high moral principles in others
- Demonstrate and support authentic learning for yourself and others

Respect
- Consider each action as a chance to gain trust
- Create a community that values learning and learners
- Demonstrate self-respect

Trust
- Proven demonstration of integrity that can be relied upon
- Ability to give responsibility to others and believe the task will be performed with integrity

Responsibility
- Accomplish what you commit to do
- Be willing to own what you do and say
- Embrace and advance the common good of our community
- Have the courage to do what is right[4]

Fairness

- Demonstrate equity to all with decisions free from injustice
- Resist behaviors that do not provide equal access to resources and information

Our core values support the fundamental beliefs underlying and reflected in the honor policy and include

- That trust in a person is a positive force in making that person worthy of trust;
- That every student has the right to live in an academic environment that is free from the injustices caused by any form of intellectual dishonesty; and
- That the honesty and integrity of all members of the school community contribute to its quest for authentic learning.

We recognize that there are a variety of pressures or temptations that students cite as justification for cheating. These justifications are known to include time constraints, parental or college expectations for grades, the actions of peers, accusations of poor instruction, lack of preparation, and lack of interest. This honor policy rejects these justifications and seeks to establish the value of honest learning above grades and communicate to students that their best and honest effort is expected. Academic dishonesty in any form detracts from the value and purpose of education and undermines relationships between teachers and students and between students.[5]

Definition of Academic Dishonesty

Cheating: "Cheating is defined as a dishonest violation of rules or giving or receiving unauthorized information in academic, extracurricular or other school work, so as to give an unfair advantage" (*American Heritage Dictionary*, 3rd ed.). With regard to academic performance, conduct that constitutes cheating or the intention to cheat includes, but is not limited to, the following examples:

- Unpermitted collaboration on assigned work, or work submitted by any student, including but not limited to papers, projects, products, lab reports, other reports, and homework
- Unauthorized use of a cheat sheet, marks/writing on body, textbook, formula, note card or notes, calculator/computer, cell phone, iPod, Blackberry, language-translation website or device, or any other technological device that would inappropriately enhance one's work
- Exploiting a teacher's willingness to answer questions during an exam or quiz
- Creating a disadvantage for another student by hoarding or by sabotaging

materials, experiments, or resources (books, book pages, library resources, etc.)

- Passing test or quiz information to other students during a class period or from one class period to another class period
- Unauthorized prior knowledge and/or use of tests, quizzes, midterms, finals, or other assignments (for instance, finding a copy of a test that hasn't been given yet)
- Having another individual take a test or prepare an assignment, or assist with the test or assignment without approval
- Submission of a prewritten writing assignment at times when such assignments are supposed to be written in class
- Illegally exceeding time limits on timed tests, quizzes, or assignments
- Unauthorized use of study aids, notes, books, data, or other information
- Sending or receiving unauthorized information through hand signals or other gestures, talking, text messaging, looking at someone else's test, showing your own test, or (during an in-class essay) using e-mail

Lying: "To make a statement one knows is false, with the intent to deceive or with disregard for the truth; to give a false impression" (*Webster's New World Dictionary*, 3rd ed.). Lies can be made verbally, in writing, or by gestures that are intended to convey a false impression or understanding. With regard to academic performance, conduct that constitutes lying includes, but is not limited to, the following examples:

- Fabrication of data or information (i.e., making it up—listing fictitious reference sites)
- Falsification of data or information (i.e., falsely changing the result)
- Forgery of signature on documents for school record
- Changing a grade or attendance record in a teacher's grade book or in the attendance records
- Making statements that you know (or reasonably should know) have caused a false impression or understanding to have been created, and failing to correct the false impression or misunderstanding, such as reporting an illness to miss a test date when you are healthy[6]

Stealing: Stealing refers to taking or appropriating something—such as the schoolwork or materials of another student or the instructional materials of a teacher—without the right or permission to do so and with the intent to keep or improperly use it. Some examples are stealing copies of tests or quizzes, illegitimately accessing the teacher's answer key for tests or quizzes, stealing the teacher's edition of the textbook, and stealing another student's homework, notes, or handouts.

Forgery: Forgery entails replicating the signature of an administrator, faculty or staff member, the attendance secretary, the nurse, a physician or any professional individual, or a parent/guardian on a letter or on any other document and using this document in or out of the school as if it featured a valid signature. Some examples of documents that are occasionally forged include passes, parent letters, permission slips, leases, birth certificates, proof of residence, and medical documents.[7]

Fraud: Fraud is a type of academic dishonor that "includes deception, falsifying data, and forgery." Examples of fraud may include, but not be limited to, the following:

- Attempting to pass off someone else's work, imagery, or technology as your own;
- Purchasing or selling an assignment from another person or technological resource;
- Falsifying scientific or other data submitted for academic credit; and
- Forging signatures or tampering with official records.[8]

Falsification: Falsification can be defined as inventing any information, data, or citation in any academic work.

Multiple submissions: This is defined as submitting substantial portions of any academic exercise more than once without prior authorization and approval of the teacher.

Complicity: Complicity means facilitating any of the preceding actions or performing work that another student then presents as her or his own work (e.g., copying someone's homework or allowing someone to copy homework).

Fabrication: Fabrication can be defined as the use of invented information or the falsification of research or other findings. Fabrication includes, but is not limited to, the following examples:

- Citation of information not taken from the source indicated. This may include incorrect documentation of secondary source materials; e.g., using the bibliographic information from a source instead of going to the original source yourself.
- Listing sources in a bibliography not used in the academic exercise.
- Submission in a paper or other academic exercise of false or fictitious data, or deliberate and knowing concealment or distortion of the true nature, origin, or function of such data.
- Submitting as your own any academic exercises prepared totally or in part by another.[9]

Defining Consequences of Honor Violations

General guidelines: The judgment as to whether a dishonest behavior is an honor violation will be based on these honor policies no matter the situation or the degree. Ignorance is not an excuse for violating the honor policies. Consequences for honor violations might vary and should reflect the severity of the offense.[10] (See recommended consequences in chapter 4.)

Departmental guidelines: Every academic department will prepare guidelines that describe as clearly as possible how the honor policies pertain to their specific department. These guidelines should also clarify what "authorized" and "unauthorized" help is in regard to major projects, essays, papers, tests, quizzes, lab reports, and other assignments. Teachers will describe these guidelines in their class syllabi and discuss the guidelines with their students at the start of the year. If it is observed that meaningful inconsistencies arise between differing departmental guidelines, then these should be brought to the AIC for review and discussion.

Plagiarism: See chapter 8.

Responsibilities of the Academic Integrity Committee

The Academic Integrity Committee (AIC) is charged with the responsibility to administer and advance this honor policy. The AIC will sustain its membership by recruiting leaders of the school community to include administration, faculty, and students, as well as parents and other interested community members.

The AIC will write and implement a strategic plan to organize its activities to sustain the following:

- Community engagement in the shared responsibility of supporting academic integrity through the membership and/or participation in the activities of the AIC
- Core values of the school community by regularly clarifying and articulating values that support the advancement of academic integrity and the recognition of cheating as an ethical/moral issue
- Commitments of the school community to sustain the AIC and strategies the AIC uses to cultivate and maintain student and adult support for academic integrity as part of the school's mission
- Curriculum of the school and how it focuses students on mastery learning, which includes the respect for personal intellectual growth, the protection of intellectual property, and the ability to make ethical/moral judgments

The AIC should meet monthly as a full committee to advance its strategic plan.

Responsibilities of Others

Each **STUDENT** will maintain and support academic integrity by:

- Completing all assigned work, activities, and tests in an honorable way that avoids all cheating, lying, and stealing
- Understanding the school-wide academic honor code policy and individual teacher assignment guidelines
- Clarifying with the instructor anything that may be unclear about an assignment, with respect to how the academic honor code may apply to it
- Participating in the further development of the academic honor code during the student's high school career
- Encouraging other students to make appropriate use of their work
- Maintaining records of research notes, outlines, rough drafts, and reference works to validate individual effort
- Seeking supplemental assistance from teachers, parents, or peers to understand lessons and assignments[11]

Each **TEACHER** will:

- Present the school-wide academic honor code principles, in some clear, written form, to show how they apply to the class, including guidelines for working on assignments in that class
- Support the school's core values that prioritize student learning over letter grades
- Make assignments relevant to academic advancement and life
- Teach the process of learning and creating academic products while providing sufficient time for products to be competed
- Include mini-deadlines for academic products that could include (for example) thesis statements, research notes, outlines, and drafts
- Be accessible outside of class for students to seek help with questions and other learning needs
- Collaborate with other teachers and departments to avoid multiple large projects coming due at the same time
- Report (to an administrator and school counselor) violations of the academic honor code that are serious enough to have incurred discipline in the class, and following through on the directives of the administrator
- Maintain the integrity of the testing process
- Explain the use of permissible study aids—including tutors—in coursework
- Check student papers for plagiarism
- Encourage students to make appropriate use of their work
- Use the evaluation/testing process as a teaching strategy (recognize all test prep, exams, and exam results as teaching opportunities)
- Evaluate and test what is taught

Each **ADMINISTRATOR** will:
- Make a copy of the school's academic honor code available to all students, teachers, and parents
- Facilitate ongoing conversations and reflection about the academic honor code
- Administer fair and consistent consequences for offenses of the academic honor code
- Maintain records of academic honor code offenses
- Report "de-identified" (confidential) violations of the academic honor code to the Honor Council to be used as a tool for further teaching and reflection about academic honor
- Encourage students to make appropriate use of their work
- Support the academic Honor Committee with an annual budget

Each **PARENT/GUARDIAN** will:
- Become knowledgeable about the school-wide academic honor code and guidelines for individual teachers' classes
- Help the student understand that the parent values academic honor and expects the student to comply with the school's rules of academic honor
- Support the imposition of consequences if the academic honor code is violated
- Encourage students to make appropriate use of their work

Each member of the **HONOR COUNCIL** (see chapter 4) will:
- Organize education sessions, to be held every fall and throughout the school year, to help all students understand the academic honor code, suggest ways to act honorably in difficult situations, and provide a forum through which students can contribute their comments and questions to the ongoing discussion about academic honor
- Review the academic honor code each spring, considering teacher, student, administrator, and parent input
- Maintain "de-identified" records of academic honor code offenses
- Maintain confidentiality
- Encourage students to make appropriate use of their work

Honor Code

The honor code should provide a brief statement to summarize the school honor policies. While honor policies can be lengthy and published in policy books and the school website and used by Honor Councils to guide decisions, an honor code is defined in this toolkit as a summative statement that can be published in the student handbook and printed on posters for classroom display. An honor code may thus be used as a statement to advance the school community's awareness and commitment to the broader academic integrity policies.

The following four honor codes are provided as examples of public and private school statements to help guide your school's creation of an honor code after the completion of your honor policies.

Sample Honor Codes

Langley High School

The Langley High School community embodies a spirit of mutual trust and intellectual honesty that is central to the very nature of the school, and represents the highest possible expression of shared values among the members of the school community.

The fundamental beliefs underlying and reflected in the honor code are:
- That trust in a person is a positive force in making that person worthy of trust;
- That every student has the right to live in an academic environment that is free from the injustices caused by any form of intellectual dishonesty; and
- That the honesty and integrity of all members of the school community contribute to its quest for truth.

The functions of the honor code are to communicate the meaning and importance of intellectual honesty to all students of the school; to articulate and support the interest of the community in maintaining the highest standards of conduct in academic affairs; and to identify, sanction, and educate those who fail to live up to the stated expectations of the school community with regard to these standards.

The honor code is the school policy that defines the expected standards of conduct in academic affairs. The Honor Council is the school body charged with enforcement of the honor code. The student body and faculty at Langley High School will not tolerate any violation of the honor code.[12]

Norcross High School

Norcross High School is committed to the academic, social, and ethical development of each member of our learning community. We feel that plagiarism and cheating inhibit a student's academic achievement and compromise the trust between teacher and student, which is fundamental to the learning process. The guidelines set forth in this policy identify what constitutes plagiarism/cheating, the consequences of participating in such endeavors, and promote the values of academic integrity among students, faculty, and administration.[13]

Montclair Kimberley Academy

Honor is a core value of the Montclair Kimberley Academy. The purpose of this honor code is to instill a sense of honor and an atmosphere of trust among all members of the community.

Honor can be difficult to define because it manifests itself in deeds more often than it does in words. We all desire a community in which trust, security, happiness, and respect are prevalent for their own sake and are practiced as second nature. To be an honorable member of MKA is to employ respect, truthfulness, and civility. While we all come from different backgrounds, religions, and systems of morality, it is our responsibility as a community to preserve the ideals that we deem necessary to maintain a beneficial learning environment.[14]

Episcopal High School

At Episcopal High School, we believe that academic and personal integrity are essential elements in creating a comfortable and trusting educational atmosphere for students, faculty, and school family. We encourage all students to extend their educational experiences beyond textbooks and academics. The School is responsible not only for developing student's minds, but also for developing character, strong morals, and social responsibility. To accomplish this goal, each student must uphold and follow the School's honor code. Our honor code is based on a system of mutual trust among students, faculty, and staff; it dictates that as members of the Episcopal High School community, we will not lie, cheat, steal, or plagiarize. Consisting of students and faculty who are elected or appointed, the Honor Council exists to demonstrate and ensure that honor and integrity are fundamental principles of our school. The primary focus is educational, not punitive.[15]

Honor Pledge

An honor pledge is used in many schools as an affirmative statement for the school honor code and policies. We recognize examples of schools requiring students to write and reflect on an honor pledge at the start of the school year. In the following pledges, students affirm with a dated signature (student and a parent or guardian) a copy of their honor pledge and turn in their signed pledge as a first exercise to their English teacher.

Sample Honor Pledge Statement

I pledge to maintain a high level of respect and integrity as a student representing [your school name]. I understand and will uphold the honor code in letter

DRAFT AN HONOR CODE

After a review of examples of honor codes, create a draft of an honor code for your school:

Review and comment on the draft of the honor code:

Second draft of honor code:

and spirit to help our school advance authentic learning. I will not lie, cheat, plagiarize, or be complicit with those who do. I will encourage fellow students who commit honor offenses to acknowledge such offenses to their teacher or the Honor Council. I make this pledge in the spirit of honor and trust.[16]

Examples of other honor pledges follow that include statements that recognize students' responsibility for others and their behaviors, statements that focus solely on the individual student, and statements that may be used to sign and affirm that individual projects are completed with integrity.

Sample Honor Pledges

Three General Pledges with Responsibility for Others

1. As a member of the Mainland community, I maintain a high level of respect and integrity. I uphold the honor code in letter and spirit. I do not lie, cheat, steal, vandalize, or commit forgery. I encourage fellow students who commit honors offenses to acknowledge such offenses. I inform the Honor Council of my own and others' infractions. I make this pledge in the spirit of honor and trust.[17]

2. I pledge to uphold the honor code of Norfolk Collegiate School. I will not cheat, lie, steal, deceive, or plagiarize. I am further aware that, as a member of this community, I am expected to report violations of this code as I know them to occur.[18]

3. As a member of the Rabun-Gap Nacoochee School community, I promise to uphold honor with my words and actions. I will not lie, cheat, or steal. I accept responsibility for my own actions and for what other members of the community may do in my presence. I understand the need for honor and pledge to defend it.[19]

Two General Pledges without Citing Responsibility for Others

1. As a student at [Montclair Kimberley Academy] . . . I pledge:
   - To neither give nor receive help on a test or graded assignment (before, during, and after) unless given permission by my teacher.
   - To cite any outside sources and receive credit only for my own work.
   - To respect others as well as their personal property and myself.
   - Not to be cruel to others.[20]

2. As a member of the Lexington Catholic High School Community, I pledge to uphold a high standard of integrity and honor by neither giving nor receiving any unauthorized aid in all academic settings. I agree to all standards set forth by the Lexington Catholic High School Honor Code.[21]

Two Project Pledges

1. On my honor, I have neither given nor received unauthorized aid on this assignment.[22]

2. On my honor, I pledge that I have neither given nor received unpermitted aid during this test, paper, assignment, or examination.[23]

Honor Policy Review

This honor policy will be reviewed each year by the Academic Integrity Committee (AIC). Students and/or faculty can make proposed changes in writing to the AIC before May 1. Students and faculty must be prepared to appear before the AIC to explain their proposed changes. The AIC will evaluate each proposed change and if it agrees (consensus or two-thirds vote), it will forward recommendations to the school administration for review. With approval from the administration, the AIC will publish the recommended changes to solicit student body comment. After a 30-day comment period, the AIC will accept, accept with modification, or reject the recommendations. Additions or alterations to the honor policy, honor code, or honor pledge will be made public via multiple publication methods to include the school's website and other appropriate information dissemination methods (school assemblies, posters, handbooks, and announcements).[24]

DRAFT AN HONOR PLEDGE

After a review of examples of honor pledges, create a draft of an honor pledge for your school and describe how it might be used:

Review and comment on the draft of the honor pledge:

Second draft of honor pledge and ideas on how it might be used:

NOTES

1. The example statement of core values is drawn from a synthesis of high school honor policies with the core from Langley High School, McLean, VA.

2. Langley High School, McLean, VA.

3. Ibid.

4. Radnor High School, Radnor, PA.

5. Woodside High School, Woodside, CA.

6. Radnor High School, Radnor, PA.

7. Mainland Regional High School, Linwood, NJ.

8. W. T. Woodson High School, Fairfax, VA.

9. Staples High School, Westport, CT.

10. Montclair Kimberley Academy, Montclair, NJ.

11. Radnor High School, Radnor, PA

12. Langley High School, McLean, VA (public): www.fcps.edu/LangleyHS/honor_code .html.

13. Norcross High School, Norcross, GA (public): www.gwinnett.k12.ga.us/NorcrossHS/ pdfs/integrity.pdf.

14. Montclair Kimberley Academy, Montclair, NJ (private): www.mka.org/page.cfm?p= 286.

15. Episcopal High School, Bellaire, TX (private, religious): www.ehshouston.org/ehs/ Honor_Code.asp?SnID=2142071367.

16. Adapted from Mainland Regional High School, Linwood, NJ (public): www.main landregional.net/school%20information/honor%20code.html.

17. Mainland Regional High School, Linwood, NJ (public): www.mainlandregional.net/ school%20information/honor%20code.html.

18. Norfolk Collegiate School, Norfolk, VA (private): www.norfolkcollegiate.org/home/ content.asp?id=7&zZsec=academics&mid=7&mSec=academics.

19. Rabun Gap-Nacoochee School, Rabun Gap, GA (private): www.rabungap.org/ uploaded/Academics/REGISTRATION/2010_11/2010_11Handbook_%281%29.pdf.

20. Montclair Kimberley Academy, Montclair, NJ (private): www.mka.org/page.cfm?p= 286.

21. Lexington Catholic High School, Lexington, KY (private, religious): www.lexington catholic.com/honor_council.htm.

22. River Hill High School, Clarksville, MD (public): www.howard.k12.md.us/rhhs/honor/ honorcouncil2.htm.

23. The Hill School, Pottstown, PA (private): www.thehill.org/home/content.asp?id=104& pointID=508&zzSec=about%20the%20hill.

24. Based in part on Montclair Kimberley Academy, Montclair, NJ (private): www.mka .org/page.cfm?p=286.

CHAPTER 4

Creating an Honor Council

The creation of an Honor Council offers an effective strategy for students and faculty to collaborate with the school administration on the adjudication of honor violations. An Honor Council as defined in this toolkit is a separate committee from the AIC and is responsible for reviewing specific cases in which the school's honor code may have been violated. The council should only be an investigation and recommendation body for the school administration. An Honor Council is not a court of law and acts only as a communication, review, recommendation, and education service for the school. We recommend students be full members of a council as a leadership and service opportunity to support the goal of academic integrity. The Honor Council may be organized as an extracurricular service activity for students and adults. Service on the Honor Council requires meaningful dedication and time commitment from all members.

We recognize there are legitimate concerns regarding the involvement of students in any manner within a disciplinary (and thus confidential) action of the school. As recommended here, there are reasonable strategies to highlight the importance of confidentiality for Honor Council members (students and adults). Maintaining confidentiality of all proceedings and one's own personal record of integrity are essential requirements for participating on the Honor Council. In addition, if students are full council members, any student who is referred to the Honor Council may voluntarily "opt out" of council review if that student does not want her or his case reviewed by peers. For the sake of this toolkit, we will assume that students are invited to be full participants in the Honor Council.

There are a variety of ways that an Honor Council can be utilized. Some schools establish an Honor Council as the first referral point with voluntary participation by students accused of violations. Other schools use their Honor Council as an appeal body to review a case in dispute between a student and teacher, and finally, some schools only use their Honor Council as a group to

I personally don't like when other students make a habit of copying off other students' assignments. When I work on an assignment, I don't do it just to get it done; I do it to get a good grade. Why should someone that didn't attempt to do the assignment get credit for my hard work? I take pride in what I do so I wouldn't want someone else to be acknowledged for my effort.

High school student

track reports of honor violations with the goal of watching for repeat offenders and alerting teachers and the administration when these cases arise.

The following narrative will describe the most proactive use of an Honor Council as the first line of referral by teachers or students in the event of an honor violation. Figure 4.1 provides a schematic pathway of a student who is accused of an honor violation.

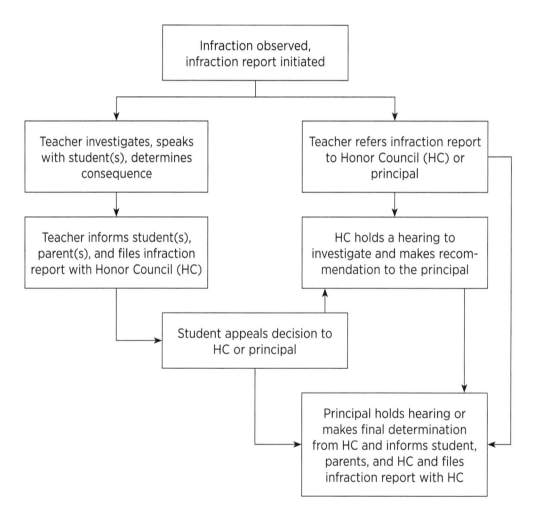

Figure 4.1. Pathway for resolving honor violations

When a suspected honor infraction is observed, a teacher or student is requested to complete an Honor Code Infraction Report (see pages 70–72). Teachers are encouraged to deal with the infraction at the classroom level to investigate, speak with the student, determine consequences, and report them to the student and her or his parents or guardians, and then submit the infraction report to the designated school office for secure filing with the Honor Council.

If the teacher does not want to investigate the matter, he or she may file the infraction report with the designated office and have the school administration or the Honor Council follow up. The student suspected of honor violation must agree to have the Honor Council investigate the case; otherwise, the case goes to the administration.

The student may also appeal the decision of the teacher or Honor Council to the administration.

Mission of the Honor Council

It is recommended that the school administration and AIC conduct a professional legal review of their honor policies, and particularly those policies relating to an Honor Council. The mission and policies of the Honor Council described here are not meant to usurp the school administration's responsibility for all final decisions as to the outcome and consequences assigned to students who violate the school's honor policies.

The following narrative provides another synthesis of policy statements gleaned from a survey of public and private school Honor Council policies as well as the work of Gould and Roberts (2007). AICs are encouraged to review and discuss these Honor Council policies in the creation of their own Honor Council.

Example Honor Council Policy

Responsibilities

The Honor Council is responsible for reviewing specific cases in which the honor code may have been violated and making recommendations to the school administration. The Honor Council will accomplish the following tasks:

1. The Honor Council will provide a confidential reporting and hearing process for students or faculty to report suspected honor code violations.
2. Suspected honor code violations will be forwarded to an Honor Council executive committee to determine whether the reported violations require the review of the full Honor Council.
3. The executive committee will inform relevant individuals of the Honor Council hearing date, time, and location and require the student(s) in question to confirm notification of parent(s) or guardian(s).
4. During a hearing, the Honor Council will seek and review relevant informa-

tion from the reporting individual(s) and from the student(s) in question of honor code violations.

5. The Honor Council will decide by consensus whether or not the honor code has been violated.
6. If the honor code was violated, the Honor Council will identify an appropriate consequence.
7. The Honor Council will refer facts of the case to the school administration and provide a recommendation of consequences.
8. After learning the administration's decision, the Honor Council will inform the student(s) in question and the reporting individual(s) of the decision and any associated consequences.
9. The Honor Council will maintain secure and confidential records of all hearings. These records will be destroyed at the conclusion of the students' graduation year.[1]

Membership and Composition

The Honor Council shall be formed in the spring of every year to begin its service in the fall of the next school year. Members shall serve for one year with the option of renewable terms. The committee shall consist of twelve student members (four each from sophomore, junior, and senior classes), one administrator, and three classroom teachers (each teacher to be from a different academic department). One of the teachers shall be designated the faculty sponsor. Faculty and administrative appointments to the Honor Council will be designated by the principal. There should be a minimum of five Honor Council members present to host a hearing.

Students must complete and submit an Honor Council application, which includes two faculty recommendations. Student applicants must have a record free of honor violations in the past nine months, must maintain a GPA above 2.5, and must not be involved in the student council or as an officer of any other extracurricular activity. The Honor Council faculty sponsor and administrative representative will make final selection of Honor Council members. The executive committee of the student council may make recommendations as to the selection of Honor Council members.

At the beginning of the school year, the Honor Council members will vote for one senior to be the chairperson. The runner-up will act as vice-chair. The chairperson will serve as the chief administrator for all activities of the Honor Council and will preside over all meetings and hearings that come before the council. Similarly, council members will elect one member from the junior class and one member from the sophomore class to serve on the council's executive committee along with the faculty sponsor and administrator.

At the first Honor Council meeting, council members will affirm the honor pledge and agree to inform the council of any personal violations of the honor code. If, at any time, a member of the Honor Council is found guilty of a violation or suspended from school, that individual will be immediately dismissed from the council. He or she will be replaced through a reopening of the Honor Council application process. Honor Council members are expected to be role models, follow school rules, and uphold the principles and values of the honor code.[2]

Confidentiality

All Honor Council members must sign a Pledge of Confidentiality at the beginning of each school year and recite the Pledge of Confidentiality at the beginning of each meeting. The members must understand and respect the need for confidentiality concerning all cases and the details surrounding these cases. Council members are not allowed to discuss cases or their deliberations or recommendations about any case with anyone beyond the realm of the Honor Council meeting.

- An Honor Council member who is found to have discussed council cases outside of an Honor Council meeting with anyone not on the council or specifically designated by the school principal will be dismissed from the council.
- All records of the Honor Council are placed in a secure and confidential file maintained by the school administration until the students in violation of the honor code graduate.
- The Pledge of Confidentiality: *I pledge to keep any names and/or case information that I obtain through Honor Council meetings in the strictest of confidence. I promise not to discuss any aspects of Honor Council cases with anyone outside the Honor Council other than those designated by the school administration.*[3]

Referral

A teacher or student can complete an Honor Code Infraction Report (see pages 70–72) and turn it in to the principal's (or other designated administrator) office, if a student is suspected of violating the honor code. Students can make their referrals anonymously or identify themselves as witnesses. Teachers should inform the student in question if they are making an infraction report and, where possible, attempt to resolve the issue at the classroom level. The student in question should be instructed to avoid discussing the referral beyond informing his or her parents or seeking counsel from another school faculty member whom he or she can choose as an advisor.

Regardless of how an infraction is resolved at the classroom level, teachers are requested to file all infraction reports with the designated administrative office for filing by the Honor Council. This process assures tracking of honor code infractions that may occur with the same student in different years or classes. The principal (or designated administrator) will refer the infraction report on to the Honor Council sponsor if the alleged violator agrees to a review. If the alleged violator does not agree to a review by the Honor Council, the designated administrator will review and decide the outcome for the infraction.

The Honor Council sponsor will convene the Honor Council executive committee within two school days of receiving an Honor Code Infraction Report. The executive committee will complete a preliminary review to determine whether the referral process should continue. The decision to follow up on the referral must be communicated to the reporting party (teacher or student, if known) within two school days of receipt by the Honor Council. If the executive committee believes there is evidence of an honor code violation, the student suspected of the violation will be given a copy of the referral in order to complete her or his response. The student must return a referral form with a written response to the question of an honor code violation along with a parent/guardian signature on the form to the Honor Council sponsor within two school days.

The student will also choose to mark one of five options on the referral form:

- Acknowledge that he or she violated the honor code and accept the consequences chosen by the teacher without further review.

- Acknowledge that he or she violated the honor code and accept the penalty recommended by the Honor Council executive committee without the principal's review.

- Acknowledge that he or she violated the honor code and accept the penalty recommended by the Honor Council; however, the student requests the opportunity to speak to the Honor Council before a final penalty is assigned without the principal's review.

- Maintain that he or she did not violate the honor code and request that an investigation and hearing be conducted by the Honor Council with findings and recommendation submitted to the principal.

- Maintain that he or she did not violate the honor code and request that an investigation and hearing be conducted by the principal.[4]

If requested, the Honor Council will schedule a date and time to hear the student's case, and submit its recommendations to the principal for the final decision. The hearing cannot be scheduled without the student in question's returned referral form signed by her or his parent(s) or guardian(s). Honor Council members may recuse themselves if they believe a unique relationship with a reporting party or student in question might compromise their ability to make a fair recommendation.

Hearing Procedures

- The Honor Council chair welcomes all participants to a hearing that may include the reporting individual(s) and student(s) in question and their faculty advisor(s).
- The Honor Council restates its Confidentiality Pledge and encourages all present to honor the pledge.
- An executive committee member explains the case to all present and reads all statements on the referral form.
- All but the Honor Council are excused from the hearing room, and then those excused individually return to present additional observations and respond to questions from the council.
- The student in question is invited to give her or his statement in the presence of her or his advisor, and follow-up questions from the Honor Council are heard.
- The student in question is dismissed so that the council can review the case. The student's advisor is invited to give a statement regarding the character of the student.
- Honor Council members discuss the case and vote on three possible recommendations to be forwarded to the principal: (1) not guilty and the resulting records are destroyed; (2) negligent: there is some negligent behavior by the student in question, but not sufficient evidence of intent to violate the honor code, or the violation is minor—the recommendation is a warning and completion of an honor code assignment; or (3) guilty with recommendation for consequences forwarded to the principal.
- The Honor Council should work for agreement; however, a guilty, negligent, or not guilty vote can be reached if four of five Honor Council members agree.
- After the council reaches its agreement, the student in question and her or his advisor are invited back into the hearing room to learn of the recommendation (not guilty, negligent, or guilty) that will be forwarded to the principal (the student will not be told recommended consequences until the principal's approval).
- After the principal's review and approval, an adult member and a student member of the council meet with the student in question (and the student's advisor if he or she chooses) to provide a written finding and any consequences for the case. A copy of this finding dated on the meeting date and signed by the student will be placed in her or his Honor Council folder.
- All records from the hearing and follow-up meeting are securely and confidentially stored with other Honor Council files with the school administration.[5]

Table 4.1.
Guilty: Consequences recommended for honor code violations[6]

	Minor Offense	Meaningful Offense (not premeditated)	Meaningful Offense (premeditated)
First	50% off assignment; offer to redo for full credit; written reflection assignment for teacher	0% on assignment; offer to redo for 50% credit; nine-month probation for Honor Council or Honor Societies; written reflection assignment for teacher	0% on assignment; nine-month probation for Honor Council or Honor Societies; written reflection assignment for teacher
Second	0% on assignment; offer to redo for 50% credit; nine-month probation for Honor Council or Honor Societies; written reflection assignment for Honor Council	0% on assignment; disqualification for Honor Council or Honor Societies; 30-day suspension from all extra-curricular activities; written reflection assignment for teacher	0% on assignment; disqualification for Honor Council or Honor Societies; 30-day suspension from all extra-curricular activities; 10 hours of community service; written reflection assignment for Honor Council
Third	0% on assignment; disqualification from Honor Council or Honor Societies; 30-day suspension of all extra-curricular activities; apology letter to instructor	0% on assignment; 45-day suspension from all extra-curricular activities; 10 hours of community service; written reflection assignment for Honor Council	0% on assignment; 45-day suspension from all extra-curricular activities; 10 hours of community service; 2-day in-house suspension; written reflection assignment for principal and possible loss of honors or AP course participation
Fourth	0% on assignment; 45-day suspension of all extra-curricular activities; 10 hours of community service; reflection paper to Honor Council	0% on assignment; 45-day suspension from all extra-curricular activities; 10 hours of community service; 2-day in-house suspension; written reflection assignment for principal	0% on assignment; 45-day suspension from all extra-curricular activities; 20 hours of community service, 2-day out-of-school suspension; loss of honors or AP course participation; written reflection assignment for principal

Consequences

Finding of Negligence: The Honor Council will assign a reflective activity to be completed in writing whereby the student will show understanding of how greater attention and adherence to the honor code could have avoided the negligent act.

Table 4.1 lists suggested consequences for students who are found guilty of honor code violations. Other consequences noted in school policies include detentions[7] and refusal to offer letters of recommendation.[8]

Appeals

The process of appealing the findings and consequences of an honor code violation is as follows:

- The student in question and/or parent or guardian will file a written statement requesting the appeal and their justification for the request within five school days of the dated finding.
- The principal will review the appeal letter and the student's Honor Council folder and meet (at her or his discretion) with the executive committee of the Honor Council.
- The principal schedules a meeting with the parents and student in question.
- Based on this meeting, the principal affirms or alters the recommendations and consequences of the initial finding and documents the decision for the student's Honor Council folder.
- The principal informs the Honor Council and original interested parties of the result of the appeal.
- All documents involved with an appeal will be kept with the student's original Honor Council folder.
- If the penalty is overturned by the principal, all paperwork involving the supposed violation will remain in the student's guidance folder.[9]

Building Integrity

The CitiCorp Tower, a 59-story high-rise in New York City, was completed in early 1978; William LeMessurier served as the project's structural engineer. A renowned alumnus of the Harvard Graduate School of Design and MIT, LeMessurier had designed banks, airports, and museums across the country. During the construction of the CitiCorp Tower, a contractor offered a substantial money savings if bolted joints were used instead of welds. LeMessurier reviewed the change, approved it, and construction continued.

In June of 1978, LeMessurier was teaching structural design at Harvard. A student from another university contacted him and said that the building's series of supports were ill placed. LeMessurier assured him that this was not the case, but then challenged his own students to work out this proposition in class. They ran computations and calculated forces imposed on the building by strong winds. It turned out that the switch from welds to bolts was a very poor and dangerous decision. If a storm set the bolts loose on the thirtieth floor, the entire building would come tumbling down. LeMessurier noted, "I made all these calculations, then stopped and said, 'This is real bad.' I made up my mind right then and there; I'll have to do something about it. I cannot live the rest of my life just waiting for this building to fall down."

HONOR CODE INFRACTION REPORT

This report is to be completed by the reporting teacher and forwarded to school office.

Date: _____

Student name: _____ Year of graduation class: _____

Teacher name: _____ Course: _____

Teacher is seeking additional follow-up on this infraction: Yes _____   No _____

Teacher has spoken directly with student: Yes _____   No _____

Teacher has communicated with parent: Yes _____   No _____

If yes, parent contact information: _____

Student Response (check one)
- ☐ Student acknowledges that he/she violated the honor code and accepts the consequences chosen by the teacher without further review.
- ☐ Student acknowledges that he/she violated the honor code, requests Honor Council review, and will accept the penalty recommended by the Honor Council Executive Committee without principal's review.
- ☐ Student acknowledges that he/she violated the honor code, requests Honor Council review, and will accept the penalty recommended by the Honor Council; however, the student requests the opportunity to speak to the Honor Council before a final penalty is assigned without the principal's review.
- ☐ Student maintains that he/she did not violate the honor code and requests an investigation and hearing be conducted by the Honor Council with findings and recommendation submitted to the principal.
- ☐ Student maintains that he/she did not violate the honor code and requests an investigation and hearing be conducted by the principal.

Infraction Observed	
	Giving unauthorized aid during an exam/quiz
	Receiving unauthorized aid during an exam/quiz
	Giving or receiving advanced information about an exam/quiz
	Using unauthorized notes/resources in any form (written/electronic)
	Group work on individual project
	Misrepresentation or fabrication
	Homework copying
	Other (specify)

(continued on next page)

(continued)

Infraction Observed	
	Plagiarism (check type)
	Use of copied text without reference or citation
	Paraphrasing text or ideas without reference of citation
	Fabricated bibliography

Description of Infraction

Student Statement

Consequences Assigned or Recommended (see below for school recommendations)

Recommended Consequences for Honor Code Infractions (modification of Table 4.1)		
Infraction	**Minor**	**Major** (infraction was planned/ premeditated)
1	50% off assignment; offer to redo for full credit; written reflection assignment for teacher	0% on assignment; offer to redo for 50% credit; nine-month probation for Honor Council or Honor Societies; written reflection assignment for teacher
2	0% on assignment; offer to redo for 50% credit; nine-month probation for Honor Council or Honor Societies; written reflection assignment for teacher and Honor Council	0% on assignment; disqualification for Honor Council or Honor Societies; written reflection assignment for teacher and Honor Council
3	0% on assignment; disqualification from Honor Council or Honor Societies; written reflection for teacher and Honor Council	0% on assignment; 30-day suspension from all extracurricular activities; 2-day in-house suspension; written reflection assignment for teacher and principal.

(continued on next page)

Other observations:

Did teacher assign consequences?   Yes _____   No _____ (referred to Honor Council/Administrator)

Did student appeal teacher's decision? Yes _____   No _____

Did student request appeal of teacher or Honor Council recommendation?   Yes _____   No _____

Attach student reflection after consequence assigned.
Recommended reflection questions
- What core value (integrity, responsibility, etc.) did I violate in my infraction?
- How did/could my infraction affect others?
- Do I have an ethical obligation to avoid repeating this behavior in the future?
- What could I have done differently to have avoided this infraction?

Please date and initial progress of this case.

Date filed with school office: _____

Date of administrator or Honor Council review: _____

Date of hearing (if applicable): _____

Date of resolution and final filing: _____

CitiCorp executives were notified and agreed to go ahead with the repairs. A plan to evacuate a 10-block radius around the building was developed and the repairs were taken as a serious matter. It was a relatively easy fix and ended up being safe and successful.

LeMessurier expected to receive a great deal of blame, and even suffer financial loss and diminished career reputation as a result of his design flaw. The press was told that new wind data had been acquired and some mandatory fixes were needed. Some reporters tried to investigate, but a press strike caused a decline in further press coverage. All in all, LeMessurier's insurance company paid the cost of repairs and actually lowered his premiums because of his enhanced reputation for integrity. He even received an honorary degree from Rensselaer Polytechnic Institute.

"I think it's terribly important for architects to learn that they have professional responsibility to the public. You are professionally obliged to solve problems and to take responsibility for your mistakes," says LeMessurier.

This account is adapted from Karagianis (1999).

NOTES

1. Adapted from Montclair Kimberley Academy, Montclair, NJ (private), www.mka.org/page.cfm?p=286, and Lexington Catholic High School, Lexington, KY (private, religious), www.lexingtoncatholic.com/honor_council.htm.

2. Lexington Catholic High School, Lexington, KY (private, religious): www.lexington catholic.com/honor_council.htm; Staples High School, Westport, CT (public): ethicsed.org/programs/integrity-works/pdf/StaplesCT.pdf; Gould and Roberts (2007); Monsignor Donovan Catholic High School, Athens, GA (private, religious): www.mdchs.org.

3. Monsignor Donovan Catholic High School, Athens, GA (private, religious): www .mdchs.org.

4. Langley High School, McLean, VA (public): www.fcps.edu/LangleyHS/honor_code .html.

5. Gould and Roberts (2007); Monsignor Donovan Catholic High School, Athens, GA (private, religious): www.mdchs.org; Lexington Catholic High School, Lexington, KY (private, religious): www.lexingtoncatholic.com/honor_council.htm.

6. Mainland Regional High School, Linwood, NJ (public): www.mainlandregional.net/school%20information/honor%20code.html; Woodside High School, Woodside, CA (public): www.woodsidehs.org/-common/pdf.php?u=1397; Lexington Catholic High, Lexington, KY (private, religious): www.lexingtoncatholic.com/honor_council .htm; Radnor High School, Radnor, PA (public): radnortsd.schoolwires.com/60020315 135951217/lib/60020315135951217/honor_code_07aug30.pdf; Montclair Kimberley

Academy, Montclair, NJ (private): www.mka.org/page.cfm?p=286; Langley High School, McLean, VA (public): www.fcps.edu/LangleyHS/honor_code.html.

7. Montclair Kimberley Academy, Montclair, NJ (private): www.mka.org/page.cfm?p= 286.

8. John Marshall High School, Los Angeles, CA (public): www.johnmarshallhs.org/academic_policies.jsp.

9. Mainland Regional High School, Linwood, NJ (public): www.mainlandregional.net/school%20information/honor%20code.html; Langley High School, McLean, VA (public): www.fcps.edu/LangleyHS/honor_code.html.

COMMUNITY and CULTURE

CHAPTER 5

Activities to Promote Awareness and Commitment to Academic Integrity

Cheating is wrong and morally unethical and though it may not affect you while you are cheating, it'll come back to bite you. Cheaters never prosper.

High school student

An Academic Integrity Committee (AIC) has a variety of ways to increase aware-ness and commitment to student and faculty behaviors that support academic integrity. With the creation or editing of baseline narratives described in chap-ters 2 and 3, an AIC can begin to market and promote its mission. This is analo-gous to a business seeking to win more market share of its community. The AIC's goal should be to move a super majority (greater than 60 percent) of the school community from positions of being unaware of or having weak commitment to academic integrity to something closer to behaviors demonstrating a commit-ment to academic integrity (Figure 5.1).

Levels of Commitment to Academic Integrity

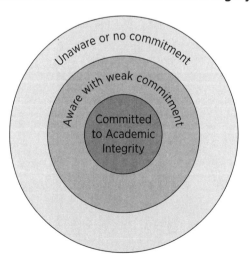

Figure 5.1. Typical levels of commitment to academic integrity found in students and adults within school communities

Commitment to academic integrity can be defined to include (1) recognizing and clearly defining cheating behaviors as violating school norms; (2) affirming that cheating involves a moral/ethical choice that violates core values such as fairness, responsibility, and honesty; (3) agreeing that everyone in the school community (students and adults) is responsible to support and protect academic integrity; and (4) resisting rationalizations for cheating behaviors and understanding that these are not moral justifications.

The activities suggested in this chapter offer ideas and project outlines to help address all three commitment levels typically found in schools. For those with no commitment or those who are unaware of academic integrity issues, suggested activities include school public address and TV announcements, new narratives in school handbooks and student planners, posters, and flyers announcing contests in the school. To improve commitment levels of faculty and staff, pledge drives, class discussions, and student skits could all be used, as well as public service announcements that attempt to connect the school community with a deeper understanding and moral reason for integrity. For those already committed to the message and behaviors associated with academic integrity, there are opportunities to engage in deeper thinking, discussion, writing, and supporting AIC activities.

You are encouraged to review the activities in this chapter and then prioritize the ideas you believe will help you best advance your mission. The CD-ROM at the back of the book will provide more aids, such as additional quotations for the "Quote of the Week" handout and a survey for student reflection upon completion of the essay project described in the "Essay-Writing Assignment/Contest" handout.

Cheating Denied

An Academic Integrity Committee member at Bronze High School (a pseudonym) shared a success story involving a student who recently was asked to cheat by a classmate. The first student simply showed his Integrity bracelet to the other person, which quickly ended the request.

The little intervention of handing out Integrity bracelets to students and faculty who say the Integrity pledge had a demonstrated outcome weeks after the last pledge drive was carried out.

Personal communication at Bronze High School, February 5, 2010.

INTEGRITY IN THE CURRICULUM

Your Academic Integrity Committee (AIC) is seeking help to identify examples of integrity that are demonstrated by people in your curriculum. Please review the following definitions and directions and return this form to the school office to be forwarded to the AIC.

- As defined in *Merriam-Webster's*, integrity is the firm adherence to a code of moral or artistic values, incorruptibility, the quality or state of being complete or undivided; it is synonymous with honesty.
- Students who demonstrate academic integrity (1) properly cite the ideas and the writing of others; (2) submit their own work for tests and assignments without unauthorized assistance; (3) do not provide unauthorized assistance to others; and (4) report their research or accomplishments accurately (from the Langley High School Honor Policy, McLean, Virginia).

Integrity can be shown in many ways:

- A student who resists temptations or pressures to cheat
- A writer or speaker who gives proper credit to thoughts or quotes from others
- A musician who properly pays royalties for the use of sheet music
- A military leader who seeks to ensure the protection of noncombatants and doesn't exploit civilians
- An athlete who trains and performs without illicit drugs or steroids.
- A politician who represents all constituents fairly without influence from bribes or donations.
- A businessman who does not exploit resources (people or the environment) and administers a sustainable and equitable business.
- A researcher who properly records and interprets data.
- An educator who correctly practices copyright laws.

Please help the AIC find examples of integrity demonstrated within your curriculum by completing the following table.

Your name: _____

Description of How Integrity Is Demonstrated	Class/Subject	Class (Grade 9–12)	Quarter example is covered (1st–4th)

Do you have other examples you'd like to share?   Yes _____   No _____

MARKETING AIC ACTIVITIES

There are a variety of AIC programs and activities that require a well-designed marketing plan to inform the school community of relevant information or the opportunity to participate in a project. Each AIC's marketing outlets might have unique strengths and weaknesses. The following suggestions are provided for an AIC to generate a marketing plan for any given activity. One recommendation is to always use multiple strategies to get your message out. Don't be satisfied with just one marketing venue such as school announcements when the school has a variety of ways to communicate within the community.

Topics	Tasks	Who Is Responsible	Time to Complete
Define objectives	• Use the activity to build awareness of and commitment to the AIC mission among faculty and students • Name the activity with marketing in mind • Include the AIC logo/motto to brand all marketing materials • Define the timeline to market the activity		
Administration support	Get approval of activity and marketing plan from school administration		
Resources	• Determine a budget and funding for the marketing effort • Brainstorm "marketing talent" on the AIC or within the school community, such as poster artists, videographers, and tech support • Identify donations of paper, copying, and website editing that might support marketing		

Marketing ideas	• Hall posters, flyers:
	  • Clear message
	  • Brand with AIC logo/motto
	• PA/School TV network announcements:
	  • Student speakers
	  • Well-developed script objective
	• AIC students sit at a lunchroom info table with posters, info flyers, and incentives
	• Announcement in student newspaper, website, AIC website/blog/Tweet
	• AIC representative announced in school assemblies
	• E-mails or Tweets to:
	  • Teachers' e-mail lists
	  • AIC members' electronic social networks
	• School bulletin board
	• Press release to local newspaper
	• Other		

Reflection/ evaluation	• Set aside time for all committee members who participated in the contest to reflect on the marketing process • Determine and record in the AIC file any suggestions to improve the marketing process in future • Keep a marketing notebook and record successful practices and how to repeat them.		

Idea of the Week

The following ideas can be used as reminders (each could also generate an individual activity) and presented to the school community via PA/school TV announcements (one every two weeks), flyers, bookmarks, hall posters, discussion starters for academic department or school faculty meetings, or advisor-advisee lessons. They could also be printed in student planners or in the school handbook or placed on the school website, or they could serve as the basis for an essay in the school paper. Brainstorm other ways to regularly promote these ideas each year.

Teacher Strategies

1. Define, discuss, and express support for academic integrity (AI) as a moral/ethical commitment.
2. Include a statement about your support for AI and your class policies in all syllabi.
3. Link student personal character development to AI.
4. Check on student understanding of AI and how you define it in your class.
5. Model integrity and support school integrity policies, codes, and pledges.
6. Teach and discuss resistance strategies for students tempted to cheat.
7. Connect with students and show interest in them—make yourself available to students.
8. Emphasize mastery goals in learning rather than simple letter-grade or performance goals.
9. Teach time management, and break large projects into smaller parts with multiple due dates.
10. Be aware of other teachers' major assignments and extracurricular events to balance the calendar of due dates.
11. Provide clear expectations for assignments that include student personal analysis and evaluation of relevant content.
12. Teach students clear strategies for paraphrasing and citation.
13. Check papers for plagiarism.
14. Provide resources that offer examples of citation format.
15. Explain clear expectations for evaluations.
16. Monitor testing times, use different versions of a test in class and between class periods, and arrange seating wisely.
17. Restrict access to electronic devices during testing.
18. Enforce clear and fair consequences for cheating.
19. Provide a pathway for students to report concerns about integrity issues without demanding names.
20. Find and cite examples of integrity.

Student Strategies

1. Identify and affirm personal ethical values that resist cheating.
2. Understand and be able to explain the value of AI to you personally.
3. Recognize and resist rationalizations for cheating.
4. Recognize consequences that cheating has on yourself and others.
5. Have personal strategies to resist pressure from others to cheat.
6. Seek to learn and not just earn a grade.
7. Think! Analyze, evaluate, and seek to apply school lessons to life—don't just report.
8. Seek appropriate help and ask questions.
9. Plan to learn, have supplies, use an assignment planner, and break large projects into mini-deadlines.
10. Learn the proper methods to cite and paraphrase.
11. Support the school honor code by encouraging friends to act with integrity.
12. Report concerns about integrity issues to teachers—this does not require naming others.
13. Join honor committees or honor committee projects.

POSTER-MOTTO-LOGO CONTEST

Some Academic Integrity Committees (AICs) have used poster, motto, or logo contests as effective strategies to engage the faculty and student body in awareness-building campaigns for academic integrity. Each contest invites students to create positive and homegrown communication tools to promote integrity. Schools have integrated all three concepts by soliciting posters that would include an AIC logo and motto. While the details of creating a poster, motto, or logo are certainly different, the outline of the planning is similar, and thus the three distinct projects are combined here.

The following outline is designed to support the planning and administration of a poster, motto, or logo contest.

Topics	Tasks	Who Is Responsible	Time to Complete
Define objectives	• Build awareness of and commitment to the AIC mission among faculty and students • Obtain posters or mottos that might be reproduced to promote the AIC mission • Use the project to recruit new members to the AIC		
Administration support	Get approval of the activity plan from the school administration		
Timeline	Establish a timeline for the following tasks: • Determine a budget and funding for prizes, or solicit donations for winners • Determine the criteria for judging finished products • Plan strategies and duration to inform the school community and solicit entries • Plan the judging of entries, recruiting judges, and devising judging rules • Informing the participants and publicize the results • Replicating the winning posters for distribution, or applying the motto and/or logo to AIC literature, posters, website, documents, etc. • Evaluate the project		
Budget	• Prizes: donated or purchased • Printing: in-school or professional printer • Paper products and duplication of flyers/forms		
Judging criteria	• Determine the size and availability of color printing requirements for reproducing products • Determine whether the products must be reproducible with school or outside printers • Establish judging criteria (such as having a positive, clear message in support of academic integrity; clear student voice; quality of presentation; and originality of work)		

(continued on next page)

(continued)

Topics	Tasks	Who Is Responsible	Time to Complete

Promoting contest	• Hall posters, flyers, entry forms:
	  • What, how, when, prizes
	• School PA/TV network announcements:
	  • Student speakers
	  • Clear objective
	  • Highlight prizes
	• Promotion:
	  • AIC students sit at a lunchroom info table with flyers and entry forms
	  • Announcement in the student newspaper (with entry forms) or at assemblies
	  • School website with download link for entry form
	• E-mails to teachers:
	  • Request that teachers highlight the activity and connect to their class integrity goals
	  • Encourage teachers to provide extra credit if the product is submitted through their class
	  • Provide a discussion prompt along with a request to promote the contest
	  • Provide a link to submission forms for students		

Judging	• Recruit judges:
	  • Students and adults
	  • Set date and time when judges can meet to review entries
	• Create judging forms to use advertised judging criteria
	• Prepare a form to tabulate judges' evaluations		

Publicizing results	• School PA/TV network • School paper with story and picture • School bulletin board • School website • Press release to local newspaper		
Replicate products	• Reproduce and post winning products throughout the school		
Reflection/ evaluation	• Set aside time for all committee members who participated in contest to reflect on the process • Note in the AIC file any suggestions to improve the process in the future • Recommend a timeline to replicate the contest		

INFORMATION BOOTH

Some Academic Integrity Committees (AICs) have effectively developed information booths to display information and recruit support during school-wide events. The booth described here uses an outdoor sports/vendor pop-up tent to help designate the AIC area for an information booth. Information booths have been set up at back-to-school events, school open houses, club sign-up days, and other school-wide events or for singular AIC projects that are being advertised to the school community.

The following outline is designed to support the planning and setup of an AIC information booth.

Topics	Tasks	Who Is Responsible	Time to Complete
Define objectives	• Create a display space to effectively communicate the AIC's mission and activities • Build awareness of and commitment to the AIC mission among faculty and students • Use school-wide events to get as many students, faculty, and parents to engage in AIC activities as possible • Use the information booth to recruit new members to the AIC		
Administration support	Get approval of activity plan from the school administration		
Timeline and budget	Determine budget for tent and posters: • Brainstorm events to set up the information booth • Create design layout for the use of booth space • Research and purchase pop-up tent • Create and purchase banners to identify the AIC • Determine a storage location for AIC material • Reflection/evaluation of use of information booth		
School-wide events	Select school-wide events to set up the information booth: • First-year orientation • Fall back-to-school events • School club sign-up days • College recruitment fairs at school • Homecoming • Selected lunchtimes • School open house • Science fairs • Other		

(continued on next page)

(continued)

Topics	Tasks	Who Is Responsible	Time to Complete
Booth layout	Determine in advance how to use the space in the booth for generic events: • 3' x 5' Integrity Pledge banner hanging from the back wall of the pop-up tent • 1' x 5' AIC name and logo banner for the front of the pop-up tent, or a tent ordered with color selection and preprinted with AIC name/logo • AIC posters suspended from the side walls of the tent • A table with a DVD player and TV or a computer that displays AIC information DVDs or PSAs • A table with AIC information brochures or materials for the current project (pledge drive, surveys, exemplar nominations, etc.)		
Pop-up tent	• Purchase EZ-Up for under $100 at local Walmart or Costco (seasonal) • Purchase 10' x 10' for under $700 in school colors with preprinted canopy and logo (example: www.displays2go.com in 2009)		
Pledge banner	Design and order professionally made banner to hang behind pledge table: • Determine budget and size, material and display strategy—for example, 3' x 5', outdoor material with grommets ($135 at FedEx Office in 2009). • Determine the color and layout of the banner • Layout and inclusion of any graphics with AIC logo and/or motto		
Storage	Determine secure storage location for all AIC supplies and pop-up tent		
Reflection/ evaluation	• Complete some form of reflective evaluation for all those who participated during information booth activity • Are any changes in setup necessary? • Write up story about the information booth and the AIC for the student paper, AIC website, etc.		

PLEDGE DRIVE

A positive activity to build student awareness and sense of identity for an Academic Integrity Committee (AIC) is an integrity pledge drive. After an AIC has drafted an integrity or honor pledge (see examples in chapter 3), the pledge can become a useful text to introduce the school to the AIC and to promote academic integrity. To implement the pledge drive, the AIC will (1) finalize its integrity pledge, (2) print individual student pledge cards and a large banner with the pledge, (3) purchase Integrity wrist bracelets in school colors, (4) set up an AIC booth or table at school-wide events or school lunches to have students sign the pledge and receive a bracelet and pledge card, and (5) keep track of the number of student pledges.

The following outline is designed to support a planning committee to successfully complete an integrity pledge drive:

Topics	Tasks	Who Is Responsible	Time to Complete
Define objectives	• Build awareness of and commitment to the AIC mission among faculty and students • Use school-wide events to get as many students, faculty members, and parents to sign the pledge • Continue to recruit new members to the AIC		
Administration support	Get approval of activity plan from the school administration		
Timeline	Determine timeline: • Events to set up pledge table or booth • Creation of pledge banner • Creation of pledge cards • Ordering Integrity bracelets • Reflection/evaluation of pledge drive		
School-wide events	Select school-wide events to set up pledge table: • First-year orientation • Fall parent days/evenings • Homecoming • Selected lunch times • Other		
Pledge banner	Design and order a professionally made banner to hang behind the pledge table: • Determine budget and size, material and display strategy—for example, 3′ x 5′, outdoor material with grommets ($135 at FedEx Office in 2009) • Determine the color and layout of the banner • Layout and inclusion of any graphics with the AIC logo and/or motto		

(continued on next page)

(continued)

Topics	Tasks	Who Is Responsible	Time to Complete
Pledge cards	• Determine the budget and size—for example, business-card size ($50/1,000 at FedEx Office in 2009) • Determine the color and layout with pledge on card and the AIC logo/motto • Determine the number of cards to order		
Pledge bracelets	• Determine the budget and number of silicone bracelets to order (one online supplier sold these at a rate of $79 for 1,000 in 2009) • Determine the color and statement (example: *Integrity*)		

Table/booth layout	• Determine the layout of the table and booth with other information that you want to make available:
	  • Student surveys
	  • AIC flyers
	  • Sign-up sheet for AIC
	  • Any electronic needs (music/video)
	  • Record keeping for those who take the pledge
	• Schedule who will set up the table, who will be present during the event, who will be in charge of takedown, cleanup, and storage of AIC materials		

Reflection/ evaluation	• Complete some form of reflective evaluation for all those who participate in pledge drive • If the drive were to be repeated, should there be any changes in operation? • Write up a story about the pledge drive for student paper, AIC website, etc.		

T-SHIRT PROJECT

Academic Integrity Committee (AIC)–designed T-shirts can be effective tools for communicating the AIC mission within the school, and they also can build camaraderie within the AIC.

The following outline is designed to support the planning and implementation of a T-shirt project:

Topics	Tasks	Who Is Responsible	Time to Complete
Define objectives	• Build awareness of the AIC mission among faculty and students • Use the project to recruit new members to AIC		
Administration support	Get approval of the activity plan from the school administration		
Timeline	Establish a timeline for the following tasks: • Determine budget • Determine who will receive or be offered a chance to purchase T-shirts • Design and purchase T-shirts • Plan events to give, sell, and wear T-shirts • Evaluate the project		
Budget	Determine a budget for purchase based on the goals for distribution		
Who	Choose how T-shirts will be marketed: • Will T-shirts be sold for profit, for cost, or given away as promotion for those who sign the integrity pledge? • Will faculty be given or sold T-shirts? • Will AIC members be given or sold T-shirts?		
T-Shirt design and purchase	• Solicit ideas for design and color • Keep the AIC "brand" with logo and motto clearly on the T-shirt • Provide choices • Solicit bids from multiple vendors		

T-Shirt sales/ distribution	• Agree on times/events where AIC members can wear T-shirts
	• Identify events where T-shirts can be sold or given away:
	  • Any time the AIC information booth/table is set up
	  • Integrity pledge drive
	  • First-year orientation
	  • School open house
	  • Exam weeks
	  • Other		

Reflection/ evaluation	• Set aside time for all committee members and others who participated in project to reflect on process • Record in AIC file any suggestions to improve the process in the future • Recommend a timeline to replicate the project		

QUOTE OF THE WEEK

Quotations relevant to integrity can encourage reflection, discussion, and increased student awareness of and commitment to integrity issues.

The following outline is designed to support the planning and implementation of a "quote of the week" project.

Topics	Tasks	Who Is Responsible	Time to Complete
Define objectives	Build awareness of and commitment to the AIC mission among faculty and students		
Administration support	Get approval of the activity plan from the school administration		
Timeline	Establish a timeline for the following tasks: • Determining the duration and the number of quotes to identify • Identifying strategies to communicate the quotes and any commentary • Recruiting teacher engagement to use or have students reflect on the quotes • Evaluating the project		
Project duration and commentary	• Determine how many weeks the project will run • Identify quotes for each week (see examples next page) • Decide whether the AIC will provide some relevant commentary for each quote		
Communicating quotes	• School PA/TV network • School newspaper • School website • School newsletter • E-mails to all faculty members • Weekly flyers/e-mails to faculty subscribers. Solicit faculty to subscribe (free) to the project with the understanding that they will integrate relevant quotes into their classes		
Teacher engagement	• E-mails or subscriptions to faculty (see preceding category) • Solicit faculty to include some form of brief weekly discussion/reflection using a quote in their classes • Provide commentary for quotes that helps faculty link to current issues and/or subject matter • Encourage English/history teachers to make one assignment in which students must locate a relevant quote about or regarding integrity from literature or a time period they are studying, and (1) identify quote with correct citation, (2) write their own comment about the quote, and (3) share assignment with the AIC		
Reflection/ evaluation	• Solicit reflections (provide a response form) from all those who participate in the project • AIC members reflect on the project to determine future repetition/changes		

(continued on next page)

(continued)

Example form to capture quotes and comments:

Week	Quote	Comment
(Example)	"Hence, the supreme quality for a leader is unquestionably integrity. Without it, no real success is possible." —Dwight D. Eisenhower	The Supreme Commander of all Allied forces during World War II and later a U.S. president recognized integrity as a critical factor for success. Do you agree or disagree with President Eisenhower? Are you committed to developing your own integrity?

Sample Quotes

1. "Honesty is the best policy."
2. "Subtlety may deceive you; integrity never will." —Oliver Cromwell
3. "Integrity is what we do, what we say, and what we say we do." —Don Galer
4. "Integrity is doing the right thing, even if nobody is watching."
5. "Integrity without knowledge is weak and useless, and knowledge without integrity is dangerous and dreadful." —the astronomer, in Samuel Johnson's *Rasselas*
6. "Honesty is not only the deepest policy, but the highest wisdom." —Charles Caleb Colton

See the *Creating a Culture of Academic Integrity* CD-ROM for 30 additional quotes. Other pertinent quotations are readily available by entering the phrase "integrity quotes" into an Internet search engine. Numerous websites have quotations for all sorts of topics.

ETHICS CAFÉ

An Ethics Café is a project idea to host informal lunch meetings where students lead a discussion of a prepared topic regarding academic integrity issues found inside or outside the classroom. Students and teachers are recruited to attend these discussions and bring their own lunches.

The following outline is designed to support a planning committee to successfully host an Ethics Café.

Topics	Tasks	Who Is Responsible	Time to Complete
Define objectives	• To develop student and teacher awareness and commitment in support of academic integrity • To keep the topic of academic integrity relevant and current within the school community • To advance the idea that integrity is important to the individual student, teacher, and the school community • To engage student and teacher thinking and dialogue about integrity issues • To highlight academic integrity as more than a rule/compliance issue—that it is an ethical/moral issue • To recruit additional AIC members		
Logistical questions	• What space/room can you use that is close to the school lunchroom? • Who needs to grant permission for the event and for the use of space? • Does the space need to be reserved? • Does the space have sufficient seating/tables? • Will you supply any food or drinks as incentive to attend? • Do you want to solicit a sponsor for any incentives (food/drink/door prize)? • What dates will you be able to host your Ethics Café? • Who will be moderating the discussion? A student, teacher, integrity committee member, or other student leader? (A student moderator is recommended.) • What moderating skills are necessary to host the event? • Who will clean up? • Who will send thank-you notes (if you have a guest, if someone donates food, etc.)?		
Preparing/creating a discussion topic	• What do you want to discuss? (Create a list of topics that interest students to host one event per month.) • Are there guest speakers relevant to the topics who might attract students to attend? • Are there opportunities to include a variety of media (movie clips, music, video, websites, and drama) to introduce the topic?		

(continued on next page)

Topics	Tasks	Who Is Responsible	Time to Complete
Advertising	• How will you advertise the event (posters, announcements, e-mails, website, social networks, etc.)? • Who will make and put up posters (or send e-mails or update the website) to advertise the event? • Where can posters be placed? Who needs to approve poster placement? • Who will script and have announcements made about the event? • Are there other student groups, such as NHS or the student council, that will collaborate?		

Imple-menting	• Who will script the introduction, moderation points, and closure of the event?
	• What points do you want included in the discussion?
	  • Are you explicitly linking any points to include academic integrity as a student responsibility for the true success of the school?
	  • Are you explicitly linking any points to include academic integrity as an ethical/moral issue?
	  • Will you recruit students to join the AIC?
	• What norms/rules do you want for the event?		

Anticipating problems	• What if no one comes? • What if the discussion isn't going anywhere? • What if participants get rude?		
Reflection/ evaluation	• Design and provide some feedback form to all event participants to respond to the AIC • Plan time for AIC leaders to discuss their own observations and those of the participants		

The Ethics Café is adapted from information provided by the Radnor High School Honor Council, Radnor, PA.

ESSAY-WRITING ASSIGNMENT/CONTEST

An essay-writing activity can deepen student understanding and commitment to academic integrity. An essay assignment focused on integrity and integrated into the regular writing curriculum is the best way to implement this strategy. If such an assignment is not possible, then an Academic Integrity Committee (AIC) can implement its own integrity essay contest to advance the integrity theme school-wide and provide a publishing opportunity for student writers.

Completing an integrity essay linked to literature or as a stand-alone assignment will enable students to:

- Learn to evaluate characters in literature and current situations by applying standards of integrity;
- Complete a writing process to identify integrity as demonstrated by characters in literature and reflect on the importance of integrity to them personally and to society; and
- Discuss the importance of integrity with peers, parents, and other adults.

Specifically, an integrity essay-writing assignment will help students "develop criteria for making informed judgments and decisions, and uphold their beliefs in order to conduct themselves in a moral, ethical and legal manner," as stated in Connecticut's Common Core of Learning for Aspects of Character. This standard is undoubtedly a shared learning goal in all 50 states and other nations.

The following outline is designed to help a planning committee successfully complete an essay writing activity/contest in support of academic integrity:

Topics	Tasks	Who Is Responsible	Time to Complete
Define objectives	• Will English/language arts teachers be recruited to integrate an integrity-themed writing assignment into curriculum? • Will AIC implement the activity as a stand-alone contest?		
Administration support	Get approval of the activity plan from the school administration		
Timeline	Determine timeline: • Planning and approvals • Recruiting prizes • Recruiting teachers • Posters and PR campaign • Essay writing • Essay judging • Winner notification/celebration		
Recruit prize donors (local businesses)	• PTA/PTO • Restaurant meal certificates • Savings bonds from banks • Tickets for movies, sports, or other events		

(continued on next page)

(continued)

Topics	Tasks	Who Is Responsible	Time to Complete
Teacher involvement	Recruiting teachers to include the activity as a class assignment: • Stand-alone persuasive writing assignment supporting academic integrity • Integration into a response to literature to evaluate the integrity of characters and apply it to a modern setting		
Essay expectations	Establish criteria for evaluating essays: • Set length (e.g., one to two pages) • The essay should positively affirm that the student understands the value of integrity • The essay should provide a relevant analysis of the literature character in light of integrity or an example from modern life • The essay should show thought and attention to grammar and style		
Paperwork	Essays should be submitted to the AIC by class teachers or directly from students (Suggestion: if teachers include the essay as an assignment, only the top four or five essays for each class are submitted to the AIC.) • Each essay has a cover page with the essay title, student name, and contact information • The essay includes the essay title on each page • No student names are on essay pages to identify the writers • Each essay is numbered on each page by the AIC to keep students anonymous to judges		

PR campaign	• Create information flyers/posters and remember to brand the activity with your AIC logo/motto on all documents. Also include the following:
	  • Contest name
	  • Why, who, when, how students can participate
	  • Prizes and awards that can be cited on college applications for top 10 essayists (pick your own number depending on number of anticipated participants and availability of prizes)
	  • Participation in larger events (for example: in Connecticut, Laws of Life Essay Program, www.ethicsed.org/programs/lawsoflife/index.htm)
	• If not done as class assignment, solicit English teachers to grant extra credit to those who complete essay
	• Strategies to distribute posters/flyers: hallways, lunchrooms, library, classrooms, online
	• School announcements: PA/TV
	• School-wide gatherings: lunch, assemblies, etc.		

(continued on next page)

(continued)

Topics	Tasks	Who Is Responsible	Time to Complete
Essay judging	Recruit judges from faculty, parents, community: • Recruit a sufficient number so that each essay has two judges • No judge reads more than 10 essays (about a 90-minute commitment) • Essay judges have essay-judging criteria and the form to score essays • Judges record scores on the essay-judging form for each essay by essay number (assigned by the AIC) and return completed form to the AIC • The AIC tabulates all scores and ranks the average of two judges' scores • The AIC has additional judges to break ties in rankings		
Notification of participants	Letters or e-mail go out to all participants: • Congratulations to winners and time/place of recognition • Thank-you to all participants, noting the value of the activity • Host recognition and prize distribution during some event: school board meeting, school-wide assembly, etc. • The letter includes some reflection on the value of integrity and why the AIC implemented the activity		
Publication of essays	• The AIC publishes an anthology of selected essays • Selected essays are sent to relevant essay contests/ projects (see earlier link to Connecticut's Laws of Life essay program) • Selected essays are published in the student paper • Selected essays are submitted to local papers • Selected essays are published on the AIC/school website		
Reflection/ evaluation	Seek evaluation feedback from all participants with a brief survey or questionnaire: • Teachers • Students • Judges • AIC Summarize the results of the feedback and determine modifications or continuation of the activity for the future		

For more on Connecticut's Common Core of Learning for Aspects of Character, visit www.sde.ct.gov/sde/lib/sde/PDF/Curriculum/Curriculum_Root_Web_Folder/finalccl.pdf.

EXAM SURVIVAL BAGS

Clubs and teams are often looking for fundraising ideas that an AIC can support and use the collaboration of other clubs to continue to build awareness of the AIC mission. During semester-end exam weeks, some school clubs have sold goody bags to students (with parent support of purchase) to relieve the stress of exams. An AIC can take the opportunity to be the wholesaler of goody bags with products that remind students of integrity during exam week.

The following outline is designed to support a planning committee to successfully complete exam survival bags:

Topics	Tasks	Who Is Responsible	Time to Complete
Define objectives	Increase awareness of academic integrity issues during exam weeks		
Approval and partners	• Obtain school administration approval to market exam survival bags • If your AIC membership is small, solicit a collaborating club or team to administer the sale of bags—the collaborating club/team gets profits from its proportional sale of bags		
What's in the bag?	An AIC subcommittee determines the items to be purchased for the exam survival bags and which vendor will imprint/label items with some message from the AIC, such as the AIC logo, AIC motto, the word "Integrity," etc. The exam survival bags could include the following items: • Bottled water • Nutrition bars • Pencils/pens • AIC wrist bracelet • School honor code/pledge printed on business card • Breath mints • Small package of tissues • Small bottle of hand sanitizer • White or school colors for survival bag (AIC logo/motto/honor pledge printed on bag or label applied to bag)		

(continued on next page)

(continued)

Topics	Tasks	Who Is Responsible	Time to Complete
Timeline	• AIC member commitment to sell, or collaborating club/team commitment to sell • All sales orders and cash or checks delivered to designated person (school office?) • Sales promotion six to eight weeks prior to exams • Flyers/e-mails/robocalling to parents • Post info on the school website • Advertise in the local paper • Place posters in school • Sales conclude and items ordered five weeks before exams • Arrival and storage of items • Survival bag filling one week before exams • Delivery of survival bag orders during week of exams		
Closure of project	• Distribution of receipts (profits to club/team that sells) • Locked storage and inventory of leftover items • Thank-you notes to donors and supporters		
Reflection/evaluation	• Plan time for all project participants to reflect on the process and outcomes • Determine the date and chairperson for the next sale of exam survival bags		

EXEMPLAR POSTERS

Schools have recognized exemplars of integrity as one strategy to advance awareness and commitment to academic integrity. Exemplars can be represented by quotations and posters depicting historical figures or current members of the school community.

The following outline is designed to support a planning committee in successfully completing exemplar posters:

Topics	Tasks	Who Is Responsible	Time to Complete
Define objectives	Decide who will be recognized in exemplar posters: • Students (current and past) • Faculty, staff, and school administrators • Community members (parents, business, nonprofit, or government)		

Posters	• Budget to support production and printing
	• Determine the size and requirements for reproducing
	• Set the time frame for production:
	  • Photography (professional or amateur)
	  • Capture exemplar quote for poster
	  • Generic layout for all posters—AIC citation, placement of AIC motto, logo		

Nomination rubric	Define recognition standards for nomination: • Authentic example and support for integrity (academics, athletics, business, etc.) • Willingness to be cited as an exemplar for the AIC, on posters, on the website, in news stories, etc. • Can clearly state support for integrity. Recognize that exemplars do not need to be perfect.		

Nomination strategies	• Create a nomination form
	• Make nomination forms available (AIC members, sponsors, teachers, school office)
	• Recruit teachers to take time to announce nominations and hand out nomination forms
	• Solicit nominations at school-wide events, school lunches, and assemblies:
	  • Use the nomination process to advance awareness of the AIC mission
	  • Continue to brand all posters and nomination forms with the AIC logo/motto
	  • Contact multiple media to announce nomination process (PA announcements, school TV network, hall posters, school newspaper, etc.)
	• Establish a deadline for the nomination process
	• Clearly note where the nomination forms are submitted		

(continued on next page)

Topics	Tasks	Who Is Responsible	Time to Complete
Nomination judging	Recruit judges: • Students and adults • Set date and time when judges can meet together • Create judging forms to use advertised judging criteria: • Authentic example (testimonies) • Ability to clearly state support for integrity • Willing to be an exemplar (signed permission) • Prepare steps to tabulate judges' evaluations		
Announce winners	• School PA/TV network • School paper with story and picture • School bulletin board • School website • Press release to local newspaper • Publication and distribution of posters		
Reflection/evaluation	• Evaluate the impact of the process: • Anecdotes • Survey of students/faculty • Determine the value of repeating the process: • New exemplars every other year • Expand exemplar population (beyond just students) • Other		

A sample exemplar nomination form and an exemplar nominee evaluation form can be found on the *Creating a Culture of Academic Integrity* CD-ROM.

MIDDLE SCHOOL OUTREACH ASSEMBLY PROGRAM

High School Academic Integrity Committees have made effective outreach to middle or elementary schools in their district. The following outline is designed to support the planning and implementation of an AIC assembly program.

Topics	Tasks	Who Is Responsible	Time to Complete
Define objectives	• Build awareness of and commitment to the AIC mission among middle school faculty and students • Use the program to recruit new high school members and graduating grade 8 students to join AIC • Encourage the development of a middle school AIC		
Administration support	Get approval of the activity plan from high school and middle school administrations		
Timeline	Determine timeline: • Brainstorm deadlines of mini-goals to prepare the program • Program outline, approval, program team members, script for program, identify audiovisual resources needed/available, other components of program such as pledge signing, AIC sign-up, and visuals (posters, AIC tent)		

Program outline	Program ideas:
	• Explanation of AIC purpose
	• Define academic integrity (this can be interactive—request that students provide examples)
	• Provide reasons to act with integrity and connect to ethical/moral motivation:
	  1. Maintain a good reputation
	  2. Build trust with others and protect community trust
	  3. Avoid the consequences of being caught cheating
	  4. Genuinely learn their own lessons for themselves and for society
	  5. Maintain a level playing field so that others aren't being cheated
	  6. Respect and protect intellectual property rights so that their ideas or those of others aren't being stolen
	• Teach a strategy to make ethical/moral judgments to support integrity (see dilemma models) and perform skits with integrity dilemmas to seek student ideas regarding solutions
	• Encourage some action at assembly—encourage students to sign integrity pledge card and get bracelet, sign up for membership with AIC, or nominate peer for integrity recognition (see exemplar poster activity)		

(continued on next page)

(continued)

Topics	Tasks	Who Is Responsible	Time to Complete
Practice	• Establish times for the program team to practice lines and assembly speaking with or without the support of microphones and with or without the support of PowerPoint		
Logistics	• Establish plan and permission for logistics for student absence from high school, travel arrangements, parent permission, etc.		
Photography and public relations	• Determine who can photograph the event for use on the AIC website and for the distribution of any articles to school or local papers		
Thank-yous	• Send thank-you notes to middle school hosts and other volunteers, and encourage the establishment of their own AICs		
Reflection/ evaluation	• Complete some form of reflective evaluation for all those who participated in the program • Celebrate accomplishments • Determine whether any changes should be made if program were repeated • Determine whether the program should be an annual event • Write a story about the program and the AIC for the student paper, AIC website, or local newspaper		

FIRST-YEAR ORIENTATION

A number of annual school events provide the opportunity to present a clear case in support of academic integrity. Many schools have a first-year orientation that can be used to highlight an expectation of academic integrity by incoming first-year students as well as reinforce the policies and principles supporting academic integrity in high school.

Topics	Tasks	Who Is Responsible	Time to Complete
Define objectives	• Build awareness of and commitment to AI by students and faculty that attend the orientation • Use the program to recruit new grade 9 members		
Administra-tion support	• Get approval of activity plan from high school administration • Gain support of current facilitators of orientation • Determine time, duration, and strategy to present (e.g., one large assembly or multiple class presentations)		
Timeline	• Brainstorm deadlines of mini-goals to prepare the program • Program the outline, confirm program team members, compose a script for the program, identify audiovisual resources needed/available, and plan other components of program such as pledge signing, AIC sign-up, and visuals (posters, AIC tent)		
Program outline	Program ideas (there may not be time for all these points): • Introduce and explain AIC purpose • Define academic integrity (this can be interactive—request that students provide examples) • Describe school AI policies and any sources for policy refer-ence (student handbook, school website, etc.) • Provide links to resources for school's guidelines for proper literature citation (given in student handbook or provided on bookmarks, handouts, etc.) • Provide reasons to act with integrity and connect to ethical/moral motivation: 1. Maintain a good reputation 2. Build trust with others and protect community trust 3. Avoid the consequences of being caught cheating 4. Genuinely learn their own lessons for themselves and for society 5. Maintain a level playing field so others aren't being cheated 6. Respect and protect intellectual property rights so that their ideas or those of others are not being stolen		

(continued on next page)

(continued)

Program outline	• Teach a strategy to make ethical/moral judgments to support integrity (see the Advisor-Advisee or Classroom Activities in chapter 7) and perform one or two skits with integrity dilemmas to seek student ideas for solutions • Encourage some follow-up after the presentation (sign integrity pledge card and get bracelet, sign up for membership with AIC, etc.)		
Practice	• Establish times for the program team to practice lines and speaking roles, with or without the support of microphones and with or without the support of PowerPoint		
Photography and public relations	• Determine who can photograph the event for use on the AIC website and for the distribution of any articles to school or local papers		
Reflection/ evaluation	• Complete some form of reflective evaluation for all those who participated in the program • Celebrate accomplishments • Determine whether any changes should be made if program were repeated • Determine whether the program should be an annual event • Write a story about the program and the AIC for the student paper, the AIC website, or the local newspaper		

CAUGHT YOU CAMPAIGN

A Caught You Campaign can be effectively run to promote the variety of acts of integrity that might be demonstrated in a school community. Examples witnessed have included students correcting exam scores not in their favor, students returning lost valuables, students self-monitoring to obey rules during competitions, and students standing up for their beliefs in difficult circumstances.

Topics	Tasks	Who Is Responsible	Time to Complete
Define objectives	• Build awareness of and commitment to AI by students and faculty • Identify possible exemplary poster participants • Recruit new members to the AIC		
Administration support	• Get approval of the activity plan from the high school administration • Get approval from the school faculty to engage all faculty as "spotters"		
Timeline	• Brainstorm deadlines of mini-goals to implement the project • Confirm teacher and other staff participation; create and print nomination forms; plan recognition strategy; if incentives are going to be included, identify budget or donors for incentives; create marketing plan; final recognition and project wrap-up		
Budget	• Determine a budget to purchase recognition awards • Identify vendors that might donate recognition awards		
Spotter recruitment	• Create and print nomination forms • Recruit faculty, staff, administration, and coaches to watch for and then personally nominate individuals who demonstrate integrity		
Recognition	• Determine a plan for recognizing acts of integrity (discuss the appropriateness of your school using extrinsic awards) • Create marketing plan for your recognition, with or without extrinsic awards (school bulletin board, announcements, school website, newspaper, etc.)		
Reflection/ evaluation	• Create a follow-up interview/survey to learn the outcomes of the activity from participants • Discuss as an AIC the value of repeating the project		

CHAPTER 6

Parents and Other Partners

The Larger Community

While it is natural for an Academic Integrity Committee (AIC) to focus on individual students and faculty within the school community, it is also useful to connect with people, clubs, and organizations that may extend beyond the school. Parents, school clubs, youth-serving agencies, other schools and universities, as well as national organizations and networks, are all potential partners to help further the AIC's mission. This chapter provides suggestions for how an AIC, beginning with its parent community, can reach out to expand its base of collaborators.

Parents as Partners

There are many advantages to gaining parents as partners in the work of an AIC. Parents are students' first teachers, and their commitment to and support of integrity policies will go a long way toward promoting a culture of integrity. Our research affirms that many students often interpret parental pressure to earn good grades as the most prevalent rationalization for them to cheat to obtain those grades. While we recognize that parental pressure can lead students to cheat, many parents can be recruited to endorse the idea that authentic learning is the goal of students' schoolwork. An AIC can help promote dialogue in homes to encourage students to complete their schoolwork for the sake of real learning and let grades represent their best effort without cheating.

Parents are able to support the value of integrity in many ways. Children are always watching and they see whether a parent celebrates the store clerk's error of returning too much change in a purchase, or if an unfair advantage is exploited in business or personal transactions. The father of one of this book's authors taught an invaluable lesson to his son in high school. The dad had just returned from a business trip in a sporty new rental car, and the 16-year-old son asked if they could take it for a drive to test its acceleration. The response: "Sorry, son, that's not an option. The car is rented to me for business, and while I understand no one would know, it would not be right." Teenage protests didn't change the verdict, but the father's explanation did plant the recognition that "right" and integrity result from choices that are practiced when no one is watching. This was also a practical lesson in the application of the Golden Rule's "do unto others as you would have them do unto you," which is a basic and universal principle in ethics that helps students reflect on their responsibility to others and a "good" beyond themselves.

AICs can help support parents in teaching these integrity lessons at home. In chapter 7 there are a series of dilemmas that are suggested for use by classroom teachers and/or for advisory lessons. The decision-making model for the lesson here and in Chapter 7 is taken from *The Golden Compass for Character-Based Decision Making* (Wangaard 2006), a workbook for middle school and high school students. The lesson format can be redesigned for parents to use as dinnertime dialogues or anytime the family can discuss school issues with their student(s). One approach is to give the assignment to students and provide extra credit or homework credit if the student brings back the assignment signed by all participants. One example, "Dinner Dilemma Dialogue," is provided in this chapter as a handout.

There are a variety of messengers from the school to the home that encourage choices leading to a positive learning environment for students. An AIC can and should join the chorus with its unique message in support of integrity. Beyond the clear affirmation of the core values in support of integrity that can be encouraged through dinner dialogues, the AIC can produce other *integrity tips* for parents and students. The following points are suggested for replication and dissemination to parents through whatever media works best for your school community. Integrity tips can be disseminated, for example, on bookmarks at parent conferences, through school newsletters, in the school paper, and on the school's website. The AIC can also provide text for the principal for use in composing parent letters, creating blogs or messages for social networks, and writing articles for local media. All these outlets are opportunities for the AIC to communicate integrity tips to parents and students. The following topics are suggested for the creation of integrity tips.

DINNER DILEMMA DIALOGUE: EVERYONE'S ON FACEBOOK

Dear Parents/Guardians,

Your student has been requested to bring this worksheet home and discuss the following case and determine what the best options would be to demonstrate integrity. We want to encourage a dialogue about the importance of integrity. We welcome your participation to help promote integrity at our school. This worksheet will only be graded for its completion and return to class.

Enjoy the discussion!

Background: Michael enjoys his extracurricular activities a little more than he does his classes, and his grades have suffered this semester. His parents have warned him that if his social studies grades don't improve they will pull him from his next event. So what has Michael found on Facebook today? A classmate has photographed and posted online pictures of some of the pages of the next social studies exam. The pictures were taken on the teacher's desk when she was out of the room. What a study guide!

The Actors: Michael, classmates on Facebook, Michael's teacher, Michael's parents.

Stop! Does Michael have a dilemma? (Describe the problem.)

Think! And outline your responses below if you were Michael.

What are Michael's choices?	What character trait would be demonstrated with this choice?	How does the Golden Rule ("Do unto others as you would have others do unto you") apply to this choice?
1.		
2.		
3.		

Act! What character trait should Michael choose to demonstrate? What choice would you make?

Parent/Guardian Signature   Student Signature

Workspace

Encouraging an available and organized workspace for homework is a favorite message from schools to parents. Why should the AIC add this message to their integrity tips? Authentic learning requires resources and effort. One rationalization for cheating is the student's belief that he or she is unable to complete the work. The lack of learning space or disorder in that space can contribute to the student's perception of impending failure.

A well-organized workspace supports authentic learning. While respecting that there is diversity in learning styles, thinking that students can work well in an environment where attention is diverted by a variety of other inputs—television, Internet, and siblings—violates most widely accepted learning theory. Integrity tips to parents and students promote authentic learning and could include the following:

- Students have a well-organized space to complete their schoolwork without distractions.
- Students have space to store and maintain school supplies and books.
- Students know how to access electronic or print resource materials at home or through a library.

Students will recognize their parents' commitment to authentic learning if there is a place and resources dedicated to their studies. In addition, it is still an adult role to make provision and expect the use and maintenance of a study space. Establishing the workspace is a first step to saying learning is important, and this perception is also correlated to a lower level of self-reported cheating.

Time Management

While some students are masters of their time management, this is not the typical strength of teenagers. Adults have a role in helping their students see over the time horizon. It is as much of a developmental issue as a training issue, and AICs can support the parents' role in developing students' time management skills.

Time pressure is often the first reason students will cite in their rationalizations for cheating. We briefly discuss scheduling of assignments as a teachers' responsibility in chapters 7 and 8. Here, we suggest that the AIC can prepare integrity tips for parents that include the goal of student time management. There are many tools that have become available to help parents and students support time management. Not every student has the latest electronic scheduling device, but parents can work with a printed day planner (most schools give them to students at the start of the year) and good communication with teachers to help their students plan with their assignment calendars.

Recognizing when assignments are due is the first step in successful planning. We understand that an AIC can only help make suggestions to parents and students, but the following ideas are provided as integrity tips to neutralize the rationalization, "I didn't have time, so I had to . . .":

- Student and parents examine and discuss extracurricular schedules (athletics, clubs, work, volunteering) to prioritize time commitments over the semester.
- Student records all assignments noted in the class syllabus in the day planner.
- Student records all assignments in the day planner as they are announced by the teacher.
  - Large assignments are broken into mini-deadlines, and these deadlines are noted in the day planner.
  - Student checks teacher webpage weekly to ensure that he or she is current with all updates.
- Student meets weekly with parents to review the day planner and specifically any mini-deadlines for large assignments.

These are steps that can be taken by most students given the encouragement, instruction, and follow-up of their parents. We understand that some students need much more encouragement in the form of parental instruction and discipline, and while these interventions are beyond the scope of this toolkit, ideas for extra intervention might be recognized as separate integrity tips.

Integrity Awareness

In addition to ensuring there is a productive work space and wise time management, parents are obviously a student's best resource for many other academic needs. An AIC can be helpful if it puts some effort into increasing parents' awareness of integrity issues regarding when and how it is appropriate for parents to help their children with academic projects. We can all recognize the science projects in which parent intervention made average Alicia into a modern-day Einstein. The boundaries can be less clear when concerned and engaged parents begin to edit their children's papers. Teachers can work in collaboration with the AIC to create integrity tips that provide guidelines for responding to the following questions:

Can parents edit their student's papers?

Yes, if they inquire with the teacher and seek to have their student demonstrate what they have learned in their paper (process and content) and not what the parent knows.

Can parents help with student projects?

Yes, but the help should be restricted to helping their student's time and resource allocation and asking questions that guide their student's thinking. Parents cross the line when projects reflect the parents' ideas, thinking, and work.

Can parents help their students avoid academic dishonesty?

Yes, parents can learn the school's expectations for proper note taking and citation and review their student's work to ensure they are accurately meeting those expectations. Parents also can monitor their students' collaborative projects and inquire with their child as to the teacher's expectations for individual work.

Raising parent awareness of academic integrity issues is an important goal for the AIC. An equally critical goal is to promote ethical judgment and commitment on the part of the parent community. The suggested dinner dilemma can help students and parents practice judgment skills with a focus on behavior that demonstrates positive character. Commitment, on the other hand, is a much more challenging goal to be achieved. The parent community can be guided to sign expectations for assignments and still resist the consequences that befall their students if the students are found to have cheated. Commitment takes time to cultivate, and the consistency and perseverance of the faculty, administration, and the AIC to promote and support the message of integrity are vital.

An AIC can become quite creative in its outreach to parents to communicate integrity tips. Parents themselves can bring a variety of additional expertise, time, and energy to the AIC's ability to reach other parents and students. Another organization that should be cultivated for its connection to parents is the school's parent teacher association or organizations (PTA/PTO).

Parent Organizations

A PTO/PTA can be a great asset to an AIC. It is recommended that the AIC cultivate a relationship with its school parent organization and include a representative member on the AIC as a communication liaison. In lieu of shared membership, the AIC should make a point to communicate clearly with the PTA/PTO and selected student clubs to provide them extra lead time to support AIC events or activities. The PTA/PTO provide another venue to recruit parent support and disseminate AIC messages.

One AIC campaign conducted by a school in our study was the sale of exam survival bags (see chapter 5, pages 96–97). In this case, the AIC also partnered with the school student council that used the sale of the bags as a fundraising event. The survival bags were simply a means for the AIC to disseminate a focus on integrity during semester exams. The bags contained pencils, pens, integrity pledge cards, bottled water, nutrition bars, breath mints, and tissues, and all of the products and the bags themselves had preprinted integrity messages on the items. The main market for these survival bags were parents to purchase for their students. The school parent organization helped market the project for the explicit goal of promoting academic integrity.

School Clubs

AICs should look for allies throughout the school community. The most obvious student partnership for an AIC is the National Honor Society (NHS). As part of their mission, NHS chapters are to recognize and promote positive character along with excellence in academic achievement. NHS can be a natural ally of the AIC mission, and cross membership between the two groups is recommended. At a minimum, clear communication to facilitate the participation of NHS members in AIC activities should be pursued as NHS students are often looking for service opportunities within their school.

Student councils are another student leadership group that should be cultivated by the AIC. If the AIC is to be successful in changing school culture, the student leaders of the culture should be fully engaged in the process. Particularly if the AIC has encouraged the formation of a school Honor Council (see chapter 4) it is important to have the active support of the student council. As noted earlier regarding the exam survival bag project, the student council and AIC can collaborate on initiatives that disseminate the AIC message. It is also recommended that the AIC look to the student council as a body to review potential activities and events, not only for calendar issues, but also for a check on student perception of project viability.

Service clubs are recommended for outreach as their student leaders may find the AIC mission attractive for their service goals. The interest might vary from year to year given the club's student leadership or faculty sponsor; however, the extra hands for the AIC can be a tremendous asset on a variety of projects from first-year orientation to pledge drives.

Prevention clubs or prosocial promotion clubs such as SADD, antibullying, or drug resistance clubs can indirectly be recruited to collaborate with the AIC mission. The development of (1) a moral/ethical awareness, (2) the ability to make moral/ethical judgments, (3) a commitment to moral/ethical choices, and (4) the skills to act on moral/ethical choices could be central to the success of all the prosocial promotion clubs. While not presuming that these groups do not have their own conceptual models, it would be helpful to seek where the vocabulary and teaching strategies of these groups could overlap, particularly when teachers are sought to amplify the message of these clubs. For example, a shared ethical-decision-making model to facilitate the ability and skill to make moral judgments would be of great utility throughout the school and for its prosocial clubs.

University Partnerships

While not all high school students are going to attend college, a partnership with local colleges or universities where academic integrity is emphasized can be a useful collaboration for an AIC. Just as high school students can gain the attention of middle school students in assemblies and classes, college students can often be effective communicators with those in high school. There are individual colleges and universities that have worked diligently to cultivate their own student-led version of an AIC. Some of these have specific outreach missions to local high schools.

Bentley University in Waltham, Massachusetts, has organized an Academic Integrity Council since 2004. This council is a recognized student organization on campus with the mission to advocate and support the university's Academic Integrity System. As part of their advocacy program, the Bentley Academic Integrity Council members will speak at local high schools about the values and importance of academic integrity. High school AICs would profit from finding their own local "Bentley Academic Integrity Council" and are encouraged to do their own Internet search of local universities to research their support of student clubs focused on integrity.

Agencies Supporting Academic Integrity

The International Center for Academic Integrity (ICAI) at Clemson University (www.academicintegrity.org) is an organization that organizes an annual conference focused on academic integrity. The ICAI is primarily a post-secondary association and requires a modest fee for membership. The Center's website provides member and nonmember services and links to useful resources for organizing an AIC. The ICAI's annual conference moves among sponsoring member campuses and provides an excellent opportunity to network among professionals who share a vision to promote integrity. In recent years ICAI has attempted to make a more concerted outreach to members of the secondary school community.

The lead author of this toolkit is the executive director of the School for Ethical Education (SEE) (www.ethicsed.org), which supports a substantive website on academic integrity called Integrity Works! The website was designed to assist secondary schools in the development of their own AIC and served as the foundation for building this toolkit. As such, this toolkit represents the most comprehensive published work by SEE, while the website offers continuously updated articles, an abstracted bibliography, and other selected resources that could not be included in this publication. One critical component of SEE's work that is not contained in this toolkit is the Academic Motivation and Integrity Survey (AMIS).

AMIS has been developed in collaboration with the co-author of this toolkit and provides schools a unique tool for gathering baseline information and tracking the attitudes, observations, and self-reports on incidents of cheating by secondary students. A description of AMIS follows as an effective evaluation tool that is available through SEE.

As an AIC reaches out to partner with parents and others, it is critically important to engage its own faculty in promoting academic integrity. In the next two chapters we return our focus to curricular and classroom concerns and introduce activities for teacher professional development, lessons that focus on developing student decision-making skills and reasoning with integrity, and strategies to deal with the challenging topic of plagiarism.

CURRICULUM and INSTRUCTION

CHAPTER 7

Curriculum and Teaching for Integrity

Teaching for Integrity

This chapter represents a transition of focus from school-wide strategies that the AIC might use to promote academic integrity to ways in which teachers can teach for integrity in their classrooms. The school-wide strategies that have been presented are effective in building student and faculty awareness to integrity; however, it is in the classroom that teachers can deepen students' awareness, judgment, commitment, and behavior related to academic integrity (e.g., Rest et al. 1999).

This chapter offers readers several types of important actions and activities related to teaching for integrity. Activities are presented for use in four distinct settings where an AIC might provide resources, including (1) outlines and strategies to support teacher professional development regarding academic integrity, (2) examples of literature lessons that focus on the concept of integrity, (3) lesson outlines for advisor-advisee meetings, and (4) dilemma discussion outlines that can be planned into class lessons or advisor-advisee meetings.

Professional Development Notes

The following notes (pages 117–119) provide distinct processes to conduct professional development on the topic of academic integrity for secondary teachers. These notes provide a classical lecture outline for a presenter to organize a 45- to 60-minute presentation.

Teaching for Integrity: Steps to Prevent Cheating

Results from more than 100 studies[1] over the past four decades have made two facts very clear:

1. Most students cheat at some point every school year.
2. Teachers can play an important role in reducing student cheating.

The following are research-based strategies for preventing (or at least reducing) academic dishonesty in your classroom. We strongly encourage you to discuss the following strategies within your departments and agree to implement ideas you support. By doing so, you'll be creating the kind of classroom community that helps students achieve academic success with integrity.

Communicate and Care

One of the most important things you can do to reduce cheating in your classroom is to **tell students that you are aware that academic dishonesty is a problem and that you take the issue seriously.** These are some practical steps to communicate your concern:

- State your position on academic integrity and consequences in your syllabus.
- During the first few days of school discuss with your students the value of academic honesty. **Be specific about what behaviors constitute academic dishonesty in your course** (e.g., copying homework, unpermitted collaboration, plagiarizing from a written or Internet source, using unpermitted notes during a quiz, test, or exam, etc.), and be specific about the consequences for engaging in these cheating behaviors.
- **Make it clear to students that (1) academic dishonesty is morally wrong** (i.e., it involves lying to or otherwise deceiving others and creates an unearned and unfair advantage over others), and **(2) they are personally responsible for not cheating** (i.e., blaming others or the situation is just a cheap rationalization and is not acceptable).
- **Reinforce this message and policies throughout the year.**

Emphasize Mastery Goals over Performance Goals

Many students today feel tremendous pressure to succeed academically. Getting high grades and test scores (so-called performance goals) has become more important than learning and understanding the subject matter (so-called mastery goals). Research shows that students who are more performance oriented than mastery oriented cheat more often. Strategies for communicating that learning and mastery of the material are more important than high test scores and grades can include the following:

- **Engage.** Create learning experiences that tap into students' *interests* and make how and what they learn *useful* or *important* to them. Students work harder (and cheat less) when their perceptions of "task value" are high.

- **Challenge.** Provide students with *optimal challenges* (too easy = boring; too difficult = anxiety), and *scaffold learning experiences* (i.e., provide relevant examples of completed work, encouragement). Students are more motivated to learn and persist longer at a task when it is a reasonable challenge and they are supported in their efforts.

- **Empower.** Give students some *voice and choice* in the learning process and the products they create (i.e., select product/project outcomes via classroom decisions).

- **Recognize.** Emphasize and acknowledge students' efforts to learn and understand. Make it clear that what is most important is they are learning and *developing competence.*

- **Individualize.** Provide private individual evaluation of progress and avoid practices that invite social comparisons of performance differences. Make it clear that students' primary goal should be self-improvement (that they are getting more knowledgeable and skilled) and not how they are doing compared to others.

- **Play fair.** Establish and clearly communicate your learning objectives (what students are expected to learn and why) and assessment practices (the grading requirements and the criteria you will use to evaluate all major assignments).

Specific Strategies for Reducing Different Types of Dishonesty

Reducing homework cheating:

- **Don't assign too much.** Keep your homework assignments to a reasonable number and of reasonable length.

- **Make it meaningful.** Nearly all students copy homework and most don't think of it as cheating because it's boring or meaningless to them (unneeded practice of skills already learned).

- **Create and use a school assignment calendar.** This will help to avoid students' having multiple *major* events/assignments due in a narrow time frame.

Reducing in-class test cheating:

- **Offer multiple grading opportunities** versus only one or two tests per quarter.

- **Space seating and monitor.** Space students if possible and actively move about the room during exams with all desk and floor area clear of student resources.

- **Create multiple forms.** Don't reuse the same exam every year and/or randomize the order of questions and answers.

- **Ban digital technologies.** Do not allow students to use cell phones, PDAs, and other devices during quizzes, tests, and exams.

Preventing plagiarism:
- **Make** assignments clear and manageable.
- **Provide** a list of specific topics (and/or required components).
- **Require** process steps (series of due dates: topic, outline, first draft).
- **Meet** with students to discuss their papers.
- **Require** oral reports (ask process questions).
- **Require** an annotated bibliography (could be a process step).
- **Require** recent references (prevent the use of papers from a "paper mill").
- **Require** meta-learning essay (complete in-class essay summarizing the assignment).[2]

Detecting plagiarism:
- **See** the signs (different voice/style, off topic, mixed citation styles or formatting, lack of references, anomalies in dictions).
- **Know** the online sources (e.g., writework.com, schoolsucks.com, paperstore.net).
- **Search** suspicious sections of papers (using free search engines such as Google).
- **Use** a plagiarism detector in drafting and final submission (e.g., turnitin.com).

Confronting suspected plagiarism:
- **Be nonconfrontational.** Express your concerns and observations privately.
- **Progress from indirect to direct questioning.** Provide an opportunity for the student to acknowledge the problem first.

Justifications for Cheating and Appropriate Responses

The responses suggested to "justifications for cheating" can provide a useful template for school integrity committees to host discussions or forums. They also can suggest lesson plans for teachers to implement in academic classes. Students need to have the skill to cognitively challenge the typical justifications for cheating. Students also need the opportunity to connect moral motivations to values that resist cheating. A reasonable character-based moral motivation is to choose to demonstrate integrity. Students are also recognized to accept the moral argument for equity and fairness when they understand the disadvantage that non-cheaters experience in a cheating environment.

Table 7.1. Responses to justifications for cheating

Justifications for Cheating	Response
I want to help my friend	Discuss: Are you really helping your friend learn?
Unclear rules; teacher tolerance of cheating	Writing and implementing school-wide policies to promote integrity and resist cheating
Peer pressure—*Everyone is doing it!*	Moral development dialogue with students to discuss at what point they will determine their own standards. The old question could apply: "Would you jump off a cliff if everyone else were doing it?"
Academic pressure; have to get As for parents/society	Teach organization/time management/study skills. Question at what cost: earned an A and learned the material; or cheated and got an A but had no real mastery of the material
Outside commitments, jobs, sports, socializing, procrastination	Learning time management, how to balance activities and schoolwork, and how to evaluate time priorities
Too much schoolwork on one night	Students learn to discuss time conflicts with teachers
It's not really that bad	Reflection exercises for identifying and evaluating moral right and wrong
It doesn't hurt anyone	Discuss fairness and equity issues when cheaters advance over those demonstrating honest effort
I don't care	Encourage envisioning future, setting goals

Classroom Literature Lessons

The following two lessons[3] have been written to provide examples of how the topic of integrity can be integrated into literature lessons that result in student essay writing. The novels *Holes* and *The Great Gatsby* are often included in middle school and high school curricula, respectively. As with all the toolkit handouts, teachers are encouraged to copy and use these lessons directly with the larger goal of recognizing how the literature they teach might furnish excellent opportunities to teach, think about, and commit to behaviors that support integrity. Immediately following these exercises is an Integrity Essay Grading Rubric for evaluating the essay component of each lesson.

MAPPING INTEGRITY IN *THE GREAT GATSBY*

Main Objectives: Students will be able to define the word "integrity" and identify examples of integrity by filling in an Integrity Map pertaining to F. Scott Fitzgerald's *The Great Gatsby*. Students will analyze examples of integrity (or lack of integrity) and apply integrity to their own lives.

Class Assignment:

1. Distribute the Integrity Map handout after students complete chapter 9 of *The Great Gatsby*: have students fill out the Integrity Map (15 Minutes).
2. After 15 minutes, ask students to share what they wrote in each category and discuss what defines integrity (10 Minutes).

Suggested Teacher Script:

1. *Today you are going to define the word "integrity" by filling in a concept map that asks you to gather examples from* The Great Gatsby *in order to see the role of characters' integrity (or lack of integrity) in the book. This exercise will also ask you to reflect on your own experiences and how integrity might be applied in your life. To complete this activity, fill in and around each starburst a short response as requested about integrity. For example, on the left side of the paper, you can provide a brief description of any actions you take in your own life that demonstrate integrity. On the top of the page record behaviors that represent integrity (or lack of integrity) in* The Great Gatsby. *The right side of the page asks you to make application of integrity observed in* The Great Gatsby *to your own life. Once you are finished I will call on some of you to share your observations.*

2. *Now that you have finished filling in the Integrity Map, let's take a look at your definition of integrity. (Allow for a few students to answer, then compare their definitions to how Merriam-Webster's online dictionary defines the term:* **"the firm adherence to a code of especially moral or artistic values" [honesty, incorruptibility] along with "the quality or state of being complete or undivided."***) Let's compare your definition to the formal definition given in Merriam-Webster's. (After reading the dictionary's definition to students, continue going over the Integrity Map as a class to identify the role of integrity—positive and negative—in* The Great Gatsby *and in the students' lives.)*

Homework:

Using their Integrity Map, students will outline and draft a 750-word essay reflecting on the integrity (or lack of integrity) demonstrated by a character from *The Great Gatsby*, and analyze how this character's integrity would be helpful or harmful to the students' life goals (5 minutes to explain the assignment and take questions).

Suggested Teacher Script:

For tonight's homework, you will be outlining and drafting a 750-word essay reflecting on how the integrity a character from The Great Gatsby *demonstrates would be helpful or harmful to you in achieving your life goals.*

Connection to Final Essay:

Today's activity and homework assignment serve as a catalyst to outline and draft an integrity essay. The Integrity Essay Grading Rubric is a guide for students to participate in a peer review seminar during the writing process as well as a guide for your own grading. We encourage that the writing exercise take place immediately following the Integrity Map activity to help students attain a full understanding of integrity (or lack of integrity) in *The Great Gatsby* and how integrity may apply in their lives.

INTEGRITY MAP (AFTER FINISHING *THE GREAT GATSBY*)

Name: _____ Date: _____

Directions: Write in and around the starbursts your responses to each of the four domains that describe integrity.

Characters who demonstrate
integrity, or lack of integrity,
in *The Great Gatsby*

Actions that illustrate
integrity in your own life

Integrity

How might the type of
integrity displayed in *The
Great Gatsby* help or hinder
you to live a positive life?

Definition of integrity

IDENTIFYING INTEGRITY IN THE NOVEL *HOLES*

Main Objective: Students will be able to define and analyze the *integrity* of the characters in Louis Sachar's novel *Holes* and apply that analysis to their own lives through a group project in which the students portray a scene with characters from the book.

Day 1
Opening (Do Now):

1. Write out the following question to prompt student response and discussion: "What does the word 'integrity' mean to you? Please think of an example of how someone can demonstrate integrity" (5 minutes).
2. Ask students for their responses to the question, and summarize the main points (5 minutes).
3. Compare student definitions with a formal definition. As defined by *Merriam-Webster's Dictionary*, integrity is "the firm adherence to a code of especially moral or artistic values" along with "the quality or state of being complete or undivided." "Honesty" and "incorruptibility" are synonyms for "integrity." On the board, record responses from the class to create a working definition of integrity and actions that illustrate someone acting with integrity (5 minutes).

Suggested Teacher Script:

1. *Today, I'd like you to help define the word integrity. What does the word integrity mean to you? Using a clean sheet of paper, write out your definition of integrity and examples of where integrity applies in everyday life. Let me give you five minutes and then we will discuss this as a class.*
2. *Thank you for participating; let's hear what you have written down. Who can give me one definition of integrity and an example of it?*
3. *Let's compare your ideas to a formal definition.* [Read *Webster's* definition above.] *How do your interpretation and description compare with this definition? How are they similar to* Webster's *definition? How are they different?* [Encourage student response.]

Group Project:

Students will break into groups of four to identify how integrity (or lack of integrity) is demonstrated by characters in *Holes*. Either the teacher or students can choose the groups. During this time, the small groups will be required to analyze and create a scene from *Holes* that shows how characters demonstrate integrity in their actions. The students will be asked to use direct quotations and add original dialogue when planning their scenes. This activity will give students an opportunity to plan before presenting their scenes to the class the following day. They may use props, costumes, or any additional items that will enhance the scenes, and they have five minutes to act them out to the class the following day. This activity will enable students not only to engage with the text as it relates to the demonstration of integrity but also to practice higher-order thinking skills of analysis and evaluation (30+ minutes).

Suggested Teacher Script:

Now that you have defined integrity, you are going to focus on how it is or is not demonstrated by the characters in the novel Holes*. You will work in groups of four to reenact a scene from* Holes *in which the characters do or do not illustrate integrity. Use the Integrity Scene Activity worksheet I am handing out to help organize your presentation. Please be creative during this time. You can use props and costumes to create a five-minute skit that will be presented tomorrow to the class. Remember that during your small-group planning period you must demonstrate respect by waiting until someone is done talking before you speak.*

(continued on next page)

(continued)

Homework:

Students should continue planning their skits to present to the class the following day. Students can gather any props and costumes from home (5 minutes).

Suggested Teacher Script:

For tonight's homework, you will finish planning the skit you are going to present to the class tomorrow. While at home, gather any costumes or props you think are necessary to enhance your skit.

Day 2
Group Project:

1. Students will return to their groups to finalize planning their scene and prepare for presenting their five-minute skits to the class. Students may use any paper, props, and costumes gathered from home to enhance their scene (5 minutes).
2. Groups will have five minutes to act out their scenes from the book *Holes* (25 minutes).
3. Class reflection on skits. Take time to discuss main points observed in each skit and record responses on a flip chart (5 minutes).

Suggested Teacher Script:

1. *Please gather any materials you brought from home to enhance your scene. You will have five minutes to meet with your group and finalize any details before presenting your skit to the class. I will tell you when the five minutes is over.*
2. *Now that you have met with your group members, each group will present its scene to the class. You will have five minutes to do this. During this time, please be respectful of others by remaining quiet throughout each group presentation.*
3. *Now that we are done with our skits, let's discuss the main ideas we observed with each one.*

Homework:

Students will consider why they chose the scene and characters that they acted out. Using this and the questions listed on the Integrity Scene Activity handout, they will create a 750-word written essay in which they identify whether or not one of the characters from their scene illustrates integrity, as well as an example of how such actions are seen in their own lives (5 minutes to explain the assignment and take questions).

Suggested Teacher Script:

For tonight's homework you will outline and draft a 750-word essay identifying a character from the scene that illustrates integrity (or lack of integrity) and how this is applicable to your own life. We will work together tomorrow to complete and peer-review this draft essay.

Connection to Final Essay:

Today's activity and homework assignment serve as a catalyst to outline and draft an integrity essay. The Integrity Essay Grading Rubric is a guide for students to participate in a peer-review seminar during the writing process as well as a guide for your own grading. We encourage that the writing exercise take place immediately following the Integrity Scene activity to help students attain a full understanding of integrity in *Holes* and how integrity may apply in their lives.

INTEGRITY SCENE ACTIVITY

Name: _____ Date: _____

Directions: Collaborate in a small group and act out a scene from *Holes* that shows a character or characters who exemplify integrity. You are encouraged to use direct quotations for your skit, but also add original dialogue. You may use props, costumes, or any other additional items gathered from home that will enhance your scene. When choosing a scene and characters, keep the following questions in mind:

- How do Zero, Stanley, X-ray, or other characters demonstrate integrity in the scene?
- Are these positive or negative examples of integrity?
- How can you best portray this to your classmates?

Scene and page numbers from book where integrity (or lack of integrity) is clearly demonstrated:

Characters in scene and student roles:

Ways to act out scene and character actions:

Idea for original script to support the scene:

INTEGRITY ESSAY GRADING RUBRIC

Directions: Please use the rubric below to edit/grade the Integrity Essay. When grading the essay, use the comments row to note specific editing suggestions and indicate whether the student has A, B, C, or D quality for each component of the rubric.

Possible Grade	A	B	C	D	Comments
Introduction Background/history Thesis statement	Well-developed introduction engages the reader and creates interest, contains detailed background information; thesis clearly states a support or rebuke of integrity demonstrated by selected character(s)	Introduction creates interest; thesis clearly states a position	Introduction adequately explains the background, but may lack detail; thesis states a position but is awkwardly written	Background details are a random collection of information, unclear, or not related to the topic; thesis is vague or unclear	
Main Points Body paragraphs	Three or more well-developed main points are directly related to the thesis; supporting examples are concrete and detailed; the narrative is developed with a consistent and effective point of view, illustrating the essay with detail	Three main points are related to the thesis, but may lack details; the narrative shows events from the author's point of view using some details	Three main points are present, but without much detail; the narrative describes the events, but may lack details and organization	Fewer than three main points, and/or poor development of ideas; the narrative is undeveloped, with vaguely connected examples	
Organization Structure Transitions	Logical progression of ideas with a clear structure that enhances the thesis; transitions are mature and graceful with connecting vocabulary	Logical progression of ideas; transitions are present throughout essay	Organization is evident; transitions are present, but often not well constructed	No cohesive organization; transitions are unclear or not present	

(continued on next page)

(continued)

Possible Grade	A	B	C	D	Comments
Style Sentence flow Variety Word selection	Writing is smooth, skillful, and coherent; sentences are strong and expressive with varied structure; words are well chosen.	Writing is clear and sentences have varied structure	Writing can be awkward and sentences may lack variety	Writing is confusing, hard to follow; contains fragments and/or run-on sentences and inap-propriate word use	
Mechanics Spelling and punctuation	Punctuation and spelling are correct with no errors	Punc-tuation and spelling are gener-ally correct with few errors (1–2)	A few errors in punc-tuation and spelling (3–4)	Distracting errors in punc-tuation and spelling (5+)	
Conclusion	Conclusion effec-tively wraps up essay and provides memorable synthesis	Conclusion effectively summarizes thesis	Conclusion is recogniz-able and attempts to tie up thesis points	Conclusion does not summarize main points of thesis	

Teacher and Student Strategies to Promote Integrity

The following ideas can be presented as reminders (each could also generate an individual outline) and presented to the school community by means of PA/school TV announcements (one every two weeks), flyers, bookmarks, essays in the school paper, placement on the school website, as discussion starters for academic department or school faculty meetings, in advisor-advisee lessons, on hall posters, or printed in student planners or the school handbook. Brainstorm other ideas to promote these ideas throughout the year.

Teacher Strategies

1. Define, discuss, and express support for academic integrity (AI) as a moral/ethical commitment.
2. Include a statement about your support for AI and your class policies in all syllabi.
3. Link student personal character development to AI.
4. Check on student understanding of AI and how you define it for your class.
5. Model integrity and support school integrity policies, codes, and pledges.
6. Teach and discuss resistance strategies for students tempted to cheat.
7. Connect with students and show interest in them; make yourself available to students.
8. Emphasize mastery goals in learning rather than simple letter grade or performance goals.
9. Teach time management and break large projects into smaller parts with multiple due dates.
10. Be aware of other teachers' and extracurricular major assignments/events to balance calendar of due dates.
11. Provide clear expectations for assignments that include student personal analysis and evaluation of relevant content.
12. Teach students clear strategies for paraphrasing and citation.
13. Check papers for plagiarism.
14. Provide resources that offer examples of citation format.
15. Explain clear expectations for evaluations.
16. Monitor testing times; use different versions of test in class and between class periods; arrange seating wisely.
17. Restrict access to electronic devices during testing.
18. Enforce clear and fair consequences for cheating.
19. Provide a pathway for students to report concerns about integrity issues without demanding names.
20. Find and cite examples of integrity.

Student Strategies

1. Identify and affirm personal ethical values that resist cheating.
2. Understand and be able to explain the value of AI to you personally.
3. Recognize and resist rationalizations for cheating.
4. Recognize consequences of cheating for yourself and others.
5. Have personal strategies to resist pressure from others to cheat.
6. Seek to learn and not just earn a grade.
7. Think! Analyze, evaluate, and seek to apply school lessons to life—don't just report.
8. Seek appropriate help and ask questions.
9. Plan to learn, have supplies, use assignment planner, break large projects into mini-deadlines.
10. Learn the proper methods for citing and paraphrasing.
11. Support school honor code by encouraging friends to act with integrity.
12. Report concerns about integrity issues to teachers: this does not require naming others.
13. Join honor committees or honor committee projects.

Advisor-Advisee or Classroom Activities

Many secondary schools are implementing some form of an advisor-advisee program whereby teachers and students meet briefly in smaller groups to address topics related to the life of the students and positive school climate. Often there is a committee of faculty that collaborates to create relevant activities for these meetings. Academic integrity certainly should be included on the annual calendar of topics. With or without an organized advisory period, the following activities and dilemmas are suggested to engage student thinking and discussion. Some of the worksheets provide an opportunity to collect qualitative student responses that can be useful in guiding an AIC. Other worksheets offer students the opportunity to practice an ethical-decision-making strategy that is consistent with the goals of our conceptual model. Scheduling the following activities and seeking teacher support to implement the lessons can be an effective strategy for an AIC. It is recommended that the AIC seek to present at faculty meetings to introduce and model the facilitation of activities to encourage fidelity to the goals of the conceptual model (see Figure 1.1).

Why Should I Not Cheat?

This activity assumes that a definition of cheating (or academic integrity) is shared within the community. While cheating should be defined in the school handbook, here is how the honor policy of Langley High School (McLean, Virginia) defines academic integrity:

> Academic integrity can be defined by honest academic work where (1) the ideas and the writing of others are properly cited; (2) students submit their own work for tests and assignments without unauthorized assistance; (3) students do not provide unauthorized assistance to others; and (4) students report their research or accomplishments accurately.

With a clear definition of integrity and cheating, the AIC should also help students and faculty discuss why students should not cheat.

Suggested Discussion Activity

Encourage teachers or advisor-advisee leaders to plan a discussion time during which students respond to the question "Why should I not cheat?"

Record the students' points on the board, flip chart, or SMART Board, and seek to achieve consensus on the list of reasons not to cheat. Continue to work with the students to analyze their list and identify individual or personal reasons not to cheat compared with societal or civic reasons not to cheat. Compare and discuss the students' list with the points below. Add new points (if any) by consensus to the student list. Record comments if students reject any of the points suggested here. Forward a summary of the students' analysis to your school's Academic Integrity Committee.

Cheating is an ethical/moral failure that harms the individual and society (school).

Cheating harms individuals by:
- rationalizing their cheating, which leads to more cheating (in and out of academics) and a corruption of their own ethical/moral code;
- failing to engage in the authentic learning and mastery of academic material, and thus harming their own education;
- harming their reputation (they are frauds, liars, and intellectual thieves) and facing consequences that can be serious; and
- reducing the enjoyment of accomplishments earned through genuine effort.

Cheating harms society by:
- creating an environment of broken trust, which then limits the ability of students or students and faculty to work together meaningfully and collaboratively;

- breaking trust, which leads to more cheating as cheating becomes "normal" and the way to compete in the school culture;
- lowering standards, which can reduce the moral authority of school leaders;
- forcing cheaters to depend on authentic learners (because cheaters haven't learned or mastered their own academic work), as cheaters are not able to be as productive in society while they rely on the creative work of others;
- requiring productive students/citizens to spend time and effort protecting themselves (intellectual property, ideas, writing, exam answers) from cheaters, which is nonproductive work; and
- misappropriating the authentically earned rights/privileges of those who do not cheat.

Laurie Story: Consequences of Cheating

Adapted with permission from Ridgewood Middle School Character Council, Fox C-6 District, Arnold, Missouri.

Quote: "The content of your character is your choice. Day by day, what you do is who you become. Your integrity is your destiny—it is the light that guides your way." —Heraclitus

Objective: Students will recognize that cheating can have consequences in the real world and affect a person's reputation and will discuss their responsibility to support academic integrity.

Materials:
- Copies of handout about Paige Laurie
- Discussion questions copied or displayed (overhead, SMART Board, chalk board)
- Flip chart, paper, and marker
- Respect for differing viewpoints

Activity:

Est. Time	Activity
5 minutes	1. Have selected students read aloud from the Laurie story regarding the consequences of allegations about her college cheating.
2 minutes	2. Form groups of three to four students and provide them a copy of discussion questions or refer to questions posted in room. Have each group outline responses to each question.

Est. Time	Activity
10–15 minutes	**Discussion Questions**
	a. Do we have enough evidence to know that Ms. Laurie cheated? Why or why not? b. If Ms. Laurie did pay a roommate to complete academic work for her, decide as a group whether this behavior is ethically right or wrong. Support your choice with one or two reasons. c. If you were Ms. Laurie (and you did buy papers and assignments in college), would you regret the past decisions to cheat? d. Do you believe our school needs to do more to address cheating? If so, what ideas do you have? if not, what are we doing right? e. Do you believe students have a responsibility to help teachers support academic integrity? If yes, how? If no, please support your response.
10–15 minutes	**Synthesis** (prepare a student to lead group synthesis of discussion)
	a. Take one question at a time and record main points from each small group on flip chart b. Promote full-class discussion of each question while respectfully considering different viewpoints c. Highlight any consensus view and clarify logic for these points d. Capture any observations/ideas to be forwarded to Advisor-advisee Committee, school administration, and/or your Academic Integrity Committee

Practicing Ethical Decision Making

Discussing real-life cases involving ethical dilemmas is a well-respected strategy for helping students develop the skill of ethical decision making. A part of the School for Ethical Education's *Golden Compass* (Wangaard 2006) process includes the identification of choices, correlation of those choices to the character demonstrated by the choice, and recognition of the Golden Rule and who is affected by the choice.

LAURIE STORY: CONSEQUENCES WITH CHEATING

The name of Paige Laurie, granddaughter of Walmart co-founder Bud Walton, was removed from the Paige Sports Arena at the University of Missouri in Jefferson City, Missouri, in the fall of 2004. This followed the public revelation of allegations of Ms. Laurie's academic cheating during her enrollment at the University of Southern California. Ms. Laurie's college roommate made public accusations on national TV that she had received $20,000 over three and a half years to complete academic work for Paige Laurie.

The allegations were made public shortly after the University of Missouri Arena was named after her. Paige Laurie's parents were given naming rights for the arena after they made a $25 million donation for the construction of the facility.

Laurie's parents refused to comment about the issue, noting that it was a private matter. No official word from the family or the university was provided to clarify whether the Laurie family had relinquished their naming rights or were seeking the return of their donation. Paige Laurie also refused multiple requests for her own statement about the allegations.

The naming issue was controversial from the outset as Laurie had never attended the University of Missouri. Alumni favored renaming the facility the Mizzou Arena, as Mizzou is a nickname for the school. In regard to the name change, one alumnus was quoted in a *USA Today* article as saying, "If your daughter wrecks the car, you take the car away from her."

For a full report, see J. Isaacson (November 24, 2004), "College Removes Name of Wal-Mart Heiress on Arena." *Columbia Daily Tribune* via AP in *USA Today*. Retrieved July 16, 2010, from www.usatoday.com/money/industries/retail/2004-11-24-walmart-heiress-arena_x.htm.

Let us consider the dilemma of a student, Michael, who is being pressured by his parents to improve his grades and finds himself alone in the school copy room with the science test he knows he will be taking the next day.[4] Michael should begin with step one to recognize whether or not he has an ethical dilemma. If he recognizes the dilemma exists, then he could choose to follow the process in Table 7.2 (completed for this example), which focuses him on creating choices and identifying the character demonstrated with each choice and application of the Golden Rule. This process is suggested for instruction as an ethical decision-making skill and applied to the following dilemmas.

Table 7.2. Identifying choices and labeling the associated character and application of the Golden Rule as steps for character-based decision making

Choices	Character Demonstrated	Application of Golden Rule
Steal the test and study from it personally	Immature sense of responsibility, not trustworthy, dishonest, lazy, foolish to risk getting caught	• I would not want this done to me if I were the teacher. • I would not want this done if I were another student without the same benefit from the test. • I would not want this done by my child if I were a parent.
Steal the test, study from it personally, and copy for friends	Not trustworthy, dishonest, immature regard for others	• I would not want this done to me if I were the teacher. • I would not want this done by my child if I were a parent. • I would not want this done if I were a classmate without benefit of the test.
Leave the test alone and complete his office chore	Trustworthy, dependable, honest	• No proactive harm done to others. • I would want the test put away by the office if I were the teacher.
Inform someone in the office that the test was lying out	Trustworthy, dependable, honest, responsible	• Proactive step to help someone else avoid his dilemma. This step would certainly please his teacher and be helpful to other students to avoid the same dilemma.
Inform a friend that the test was lying out and suggest that he or she take one.	Not trustworthy, manipulative, dishonest	• I would not want this done to me if I were the teacher. • I would not want this done if I were another student without the same benefit from the test. • I would not want to be manipulated if I were another student.

PLS TBL

Background: Your birthday was great this year. You received a new cell phone with lots of free minutes. You've learned that classmates are using their phones a lot during the school day. During a recent math test a classmate who struggles with his grades texted you requesting test answers for several multiple-choice questions (Wangaard 2006).

The Actors: You, phone classmate, your teacher, other classmates, your parents

Stop! Are my emotions in control? Do I have a dilemma? (Describe the problem.)

Think!

What are my choices?	What character traits would be demonstrated?	How does the Golden Rule apply?
1.		
2.		
3.		
4.		

Act! What character traits do I choose to demonstrate? What choice will I make?

What supporting character traits or skills will I need to act on my choice? Do I need to ask for help?

No Harm, No Foul

Teacher Background

Many students believe that cheating is a "victimless" crime and that no one else really gets hurt by an individual student's cheating. This activity is meant to challenge that rationalization.

Estimated Time	Activity
5 minutes	Read the following high school student quote: "Students who choose to cheat are only hurting themselves." Ask your students to (1) decide whether they agree or disagree with this statement, and (2) have a reason that supports their decision. Next ask them to discuss their choice and reason with one classmate, and be prepared to share their discussion with the class.
5 minutes	Bring the paired discussions to a close and call upon several pairs to share their observations. By a show of hands, have the students indicate whether they now support or disagree with the quote; record the vote on the board.
10–15 minutes	Divide the class into small groups (three to five students, depending on class size). Assign each group one of the following scenarios: 1. A student who has cheated on exams secures higher grades and class ranking and is awarded a merit scholarship. 2. A student has gained access to a copy of a final exam and shares it with two close friends. 3. A tax attorney your parents hired to prepare their taxes has cheated his way through school, cheats on his own taxes, and suggests some "shortcuts" to reduce taxes for you. 4. A heart surgeon who has completed bypass surgery on your father routinely bills clients for more work than she completes. Example: She bills a patient and his insurance company for four bypasses when she actually only performed two. 5. An airline pilot with whom you will be flying is hiding a medical condition to maintain his certification. Ask each group to discuss their scenario and respond to the following requests. 1. Agree on exactly what defines cheating in the story. 2. Discuss whether the "cheating" is ethically right or wrong. 3. Determine who (if anyone) is harmed by the "cheater." 4. Pick a spokesperson to report your group's discussion, conclusions, and agreements or disagreements.
10 minutes	Close the small-group discussions and request that each group report on their scenario and the conclusions of their group discussion. Make sure to have groups note where they agreed or disagreed in their conclusions. Record main points of conclusions (flip chart/overhead/SMART Board, etc.) to compare and contrast groups.
5 minutes	Ask students if they can summarize/synthesize observations from different scenarios and groups.
2 minutes	Take another vote on the question, "Do you agree or disagree with the first student quote?" and compare the results to the first vote.

NOTES

1. Visit www.ethicsed.org/programs/integrity-works/index.htm and click on Resources to find a file of research abstracts related to academic integrity.

2. Adapted from Harris (2001).

3. These lessons were written with assistance by Shannon Romagnolo and Rachel Mahler.

4. Wangaard 2006. Used with permission from the Character Development Group, Inc., Boone, NC.

WHY STUDENTS CHEAT

Use this worksheet to examine each reason that has been correlated to student cheating and have students suggest ideas the school might implement to resist cheating. Summarize responses and forward them to the AIC.

Reasons Students Cheat	Ideas to Resist Cheating
High performance expectation with low confidence of honest success	
Teachers and fellow students tolerate cheating, which supports perception that everyone cheats	
Students are alienated from academic goals and perceive teachers as uncaring and not fair or academic subjects as not relevant	
Pressure to complete multiple tasks	
Student immaturity or laziness	

EVALUATING CHEATING SUMMARY FORM

Teacher Directions: Have students complete the accompanying survey handout and summarize their responses for each row in the form below. Identify the most frequent response for each behavior, and you and/or a student can then create a table ranking these cheating behaviors from Not Cheating to Major Cheating.

- Lead a class discussion to seek understanding of the reasons behind the rankings.
- Discuss who (students and adults) are responsible for supporting academic integrity and how they can do it.
- Forward a summary of this activity to your school's administration or Academic Integrity Committee.

	Not Cheating	Minor Cheating	Major Cheating
Exchanging any information via lipreading, whispering, hand signals, notes, cell phones during exam			
Using restricted information on programmable calculator			
Working collaboratively when assignment stipulated individual work			
Copying homework from others with approval only from peer			
Allowing someone to copy your homework			
Falsifying hours of service			
Copying homework from others without approval of anyone			
Misrepresenting your contribution in cooperative groups			
Altering or fabricating data for labs or field studies			
Turning in same paper for two different classes without permission			
Using cheat sheets on paper, skin, clothing, water bottles, etc.			
Not counting errors during self-grading			
Paraphrasing written or spoken material from others without citation			
Lying about circumstances to seek deadline extensions			
Purchasing essays or papers without citation			
Buying or trading for completed homework			
Copying text from others (written or electronic) without citation			
Viewing classmates' exams with their approval			
Ignoring errors for classmates during grading			
Not reporting teacher mistakes in grading in your favor			
Altering test scores (forging, hacking, modifying)			
Seeking information from others who have already completed a test			
Turning in work for yourself with major uncited contribution by others (students, siblings, parents)			
Viewing classmates' exams without their approval			

EVALUATING CHEATING (STUDENT SURVEY)

Graduation class year: _____ Male: ____ Female: ____ Date:_____

Respond to each behavior listed by checking only one column to the right of each statement.

	Not Cheating	Minor Cheating	Major Cheating
Exchanging any information via lipreading, whispering, hand signals, notes, cell phones during exam			
Using restricted information on programmable calculator			
Working collaboratively when assignment stipulated individual work			
Copying homework from others with approval only from peer			
Allowing someone to copy your homework			
Falsifying hours of service			
Copying homework from others without approval of anyone			
Misrepresenting your contribution in cooperative groups			
Altering or fabricating data for labs or field studies			
Turning in same paper for two different classes without permission			
Using cheat sheets on paper, skin, clothing, water bottles, etc.			
Not counting errors during self-grading			
Paraphrasing written or spoken material from others without citation			
Lying about circumstances to seek deadline extensions			
Purchasing essays or papers without citation			
Buying or trading for completed homework			
Copying text from others (written or electronic) without citation			
Viewing classmates' exams with their approval			
Ignoring errors for classmate during grading			
Not reporting teacher mistakes in grading in your favor			
Altering test scores (forging, hacking, modifying)			
Seeking information from others who have already completed a test			
Turning in work for yourself with major uncited contribution by others (students, siblings, parents)			
Viewing classmates' exams without their approval			

INTEGRITY NEUTRALIZERS

Directions: Neutralizers are arguments or excuses people create to rationalize their cheating behavior. A helpful strategy to promote academic integrity is to expose the typical excuses and help students take responsibility for their own behaviors. Working in groups of two to three, have students brainstorm strategies to resist the logic of "the neutralizer." For example, some ideas to resist the neutralizer "Denial of moral issue" include:

Definitions of cheating are published in the student handbook and on the school website; regularly described in other school media, including the student paper, in assemblies, in school forums, and by teachers in class; students recognize how cheating can harm both the school community and the cheater, and know how (and choose) to defend academic integrity in the face of peer pressure.

After small groups are finished, summarize and discuss your ideas as a class.

Student Neutralizer	Ideas to Resist Neutralizer (for Students and Adults)
Denial of moral issue—"This isn't really wrong or cheating."	
Denial of victim—"No one is hurt."	
Denial of responsibility— "This was beyond my control" (peer pressure, deadlines, too much work, parents demand I earn an A, etc.).	

(continued on next page)

(continued)

Student Neutralizer	Ideas to Resist Neutralizer (for Students and Adults)
Condemn the condemners— "This is a bad teacher" (unfair, not relevant, poor instruction, terrible test).	
Higher loyalties—"I needed an A to help me get into college or earn a scholarship," or "I can't ignore my friend's request for help."	
Other	

TEACHER ERROR?

Background: An 87, that's great! You relax as you see the grade on your last exam. You didn't think you had done well, so it is a relief to see the score. That will help your average. As the teacher reviews the answers on the test, you recognize that she has misgraded your paper. You add up the points several times and it comes to a 77 each time (Wangaard 2006).

The Actors: You, your teacher, other students

Stop! Are my emotions in control? Do I have a dilemma? (Describe the problem.)

Think!

What are my choices?	What character traits would be demonstrated?	How does the Golden Rule apply?
1.		
2.		
3.		
4.		

Act! What character traits do I choose to demonstrate? What choice will I make?

What supporting character traits or skills will I need to act on my choice? Do I need to ask for help?

INTEGRITY WHAT?

Background: You have heard that several students and a teacher are beginning an Academic Integrity Committee to investigate ways to reduce cheating at school. You agree there is a cheating problem at school. The committee idea is OK, but you cannot imagine how it would work. Is a committee going to change student attitudes about cheating? Today, a friend has asked you to join the committee (Wangaard 2006).

The Actors: You, your friend, others on the Academic Integrity Committee, the teacher on the committee, other students

Stop! Are my emotions in control? Do I have a dilemma? (Describe the problem.)

Think!

What are my choices?	What character traits would be demonstrated?	How does the Golden Rule apply?
1.		
2.		
3.		
4.		

Act! What character traits do I choose to demonstrate? What choice will I make?

What supporting character traits or skills will I need to act on my choice? Do I need to ask for help?

PARENT HELP

Background: Mom just really likes to help. You are not the best at writing and after you finish a draft, your mom is happy to help you edit. Sometimes she just sits down at your computer and starts to edit the paper herself. The paper always turns out better that way. She really knows her writing rules (Wangaard 2006).

The Actors: You, your mom, your teacher, other classmates

Stop! Are my emotions in control? Do I have a dilemma? (Describe the problem.)

Think!

What are my choices?	What character traits would be demonstrated?	How does the Golden Rule apply?
1.		
2.		
3.		
4.		

Act! What character traits do I choose to demonstrate? What choice will I make?

What supporting character traits or skills will I need to act on my choice? Do I need to ask for help?

COPY MASTER

Background: This has been a tough week. Just before Christmas break almost all your teachers have required meaningful assignments or planned exams. A review sheet for your math class is due today along with an English paper. You've worked hard to get them both done and missed a great basketball game last night to finish your work. About 10 minutes before the first passing bell rings, one of your friends approaches you. He asks if you have finished the math review paper, and when you say yes, he asks if you would allow him to copy some answers to finish his page. He failed to get it done after watching the great overtime game last night.

The Actors: You, your friend, other classmates, your teacher

Stop! Are my emotions in control? Do I have a dilemma? (Describe the problem.)

Think!

What are my choices?	What character traits would be demonstrated?	How does the Golden Rule apply?
1.		
2.		
3.		
4.		

Act! What character traits do I choose to demonstrate? What choice will I make?

What supporting character traits or skills will I need to act on my choice? Do I need to ask for help?

INSIDER INFORMATION

Background: Passing between classes can be a very interesting time. Since you have gotten to high school, you recognize there can be some very important lessons learned in that brief five-minute passing period. Particularly at the end of quarters, you've seen that students will exchange a lot of information about tests in between classes. You recognize you are at a great disadvantage if you don't get the information, too. Two periods before you are to take a history test, you overhear two students discussing the same history exam they took last period. You want to know what they have to say (Wangaard 2006).

The Actors: You, two other students, your teacher, other classmates

Stop! Are my emotions in control? Do I have a dilemma? (Describe the problem.)

Think!

What are my choices?	What character traits would be demonstrated?	How does the Golden Rule apply?
1.		
2.		
3.		
4.		

Act! What character traits do I choose to demonstrate? What choice will I make?

What supporting character traits or skills will I need to act on my choice? Do I need to ask for help?

WHO KNEW?

Background: During a recent exam, you observe some classmates passing a cheat sheet that clearly has notes for the exam. Two or three classmates are passing the notes. At one point during the exam, you and another student who isn't part of the note passing make eye contact as you both recognize what is going on. The teacher does not notice the cheating as she is working at her desk. The next day the same teacher announces that she found a cheat sheet for the exam on the floor after class. She notifies the class that she intends to file this report with the school Honor Council for its investigation and not record any grades for the exam until those who participated come forward.

The Actors: You, the student you made eye contact with, students who cheated, others, the teacher

Stop! Are my emotions in control? Do I have a dilemma? (Describe the problem.)

Think!

What are my choices?	What character traits would be demonstrated?	How does the Golden Rule apply?
1.		
2.		
3.		
4.		

Act! What character traits do I choose to demonstrate? What choice will I make?

What supporting character traits or skills will I need to act on my choice? Do I need to ask for help?

QUICK WORK

Background: It is late on Sunday night. You've had a great weekend, but failed to finish your science lab at home. You set up the simple experiment and run two trials and each takes you about 7 minutes. You are supposed to complete a minimum of 10 trials and record the data in your notebook to complete the analysis in class tomorrow. You are tired. It sure would be easy to fake the rest of the data.

The Actors: You

Stop! Are my emotions in control? Do I have a dilemma? (Describe the problem.)

Think!

What are my choices?	What character traits would be demonstrated?	How does the Golden Rule apply?
1.		
2.		
3.		
4.		

Act! What character traits do I choose to demonstrate? What choice will I make?

What supporting character traits or skills will I need to act on my choice? Do I need to ask for help?

GREAT WRITING

Background: You've known about this assignment for three weeks. You've turned in your outline and bibliography, and tomorrow the first draft is due and you haven't written a word. It's getting late and as you stare at your computer you find yourself going online to look at other references about your topic. Wow, you didn't see this before—there on your search screen are several student papers written about your topic. You open one and read it and then another. There is some great writing here. Maybe you could copy a few lines just to help your writing get started.

The Actors: You

Stop! Are my emotions in control? Do I have a dilemma? (Describe the problem.)

Think!

What are my choices?	What character traits would be demonstrated?	How does the Golden Rule apply?
1.		
2.		
3.		
4.		

Act! What character traits do I choose to demonstrate? What choice will I make?

What supporting character traits or skills will I need to act on my choice? Do I need to ask for help?

CHAPTER 8

Plagiarism and Strategies to Help Prevent It

Writing a chapter about plagiarism is a daunting assignment. After a combined 45 years in education, along with the research required to complete this project, it is a challenge to distinguish what is an original thought, what is common knowledge, and what has been directly pulled from one of the many excellent essays and texts written about plagiarism that were researched for this project. So with some trepidation, and with more empathy for our students, we begin this chapter and seek diligently to avoid the accusation that one of our definitions or suggestions was not correctly cited. No one wants to find themselves the target of humorists or of a story such as the one captured by the Associated Press article "Dude—You Guys Plagiarized an Honor Code?" which poked fun at a university honor committee's "inadvertent" plagiarism of another school's honor code (Associated Press 2008).

"Dude—You Guys Plagiarized an Honor Code?"

This question was posed to students at the University of San Antonio when they drafted a version of their school's new honor policy. Apparently, the students writing the draft lifted material from Brigham Young University's honor code, which had been established five years earlier. The same honor code language was shared at a conference hosted by the Center for Academic Integrity. The University of San Antonio students failed to provide a citation when they used the identical wording (Associated Press 2008).

> **I'd really like to see stronger enforcement of cheating/plagiarism rules and more follow-through on punishments. It would be good to see teachers getting more involved in advising/working against cheating and to see strong-minded students support these changes.**
>
> High school student

Achieving with Integrity

The goal of resisting plagiarism is one aspect of promoting an ethical learning community. Ethical learning communities have been defined in the work of Thomas Lickona (Lickona 1991; Lickona and Davidson 2005) and Thomas Sergiovanni (1996). What is an ethical learning community? For the sake of this discussion, an ethical learning community is defined as a community of learners (adults and youth) who are committed to a set of core values that are defined in behavioral terms to support the success (mind, body, and spirit) of all community members in their efforts to authentically learn and grow.

Who would not want to go to school or work in an ethical learning community? This would be a great place to learn and flourish and celebrate personal and community growth. It has been our privilege to experience, read about, and visit a variety of ethical learning communities. Most recently as a National Schools of Character school-site visitor for the Character Education Partnership, one author had the distinct honor of participating in multiple-day site visits in both public and private schools that qualify as ethical learning communities.

They are places like the Lindbergh School District just south of St. Louis, Missouri, where the district administration would annually host a back-to-school lunch by putting on kitchen aprons and serving all the staff and faculty of the assembled schools. This visual act of service to employees translated into core values that the district sought to advance in its teaching mission. The clear application of core values along with an excellent focus on student learning has resulted in rising student test scores, decreases in student behavioral problems, increases in student participation in service and civic action, and high retention of faculty whom the great majority of students judged in school surveys to be genuinely respectful in their work (Wangaard and Parisi 2008).

Ethical learning communities do not just serendipitously appear. One common thread that we have observed in visiting places that qualify for this distinction is a highly evolved vision and the proactive leadership in support of an ethical community. To establish this vision requires effective administration, hard work, and perseverance. The effort pays off in excellent academic attainment, which in turn supports a high morale among students and adults.

To be authentic, these educational goals need to be achieved honestly. One objective of this chapter is to recognize how to resist plagiarism in support of honest academic work. Academic integrity must be supported by well-defined and enforced policies and rules; however, in agreement with Horacek's essay "Academic Integrity and Intellectual Autonomy" (Horacek 2009), we are seeking to reach beyond simple compliance with and enforcement of rules. We advocate that schools can strive for a love of integrity by students and adults in the pursuit of learning. This is a high goal, one that might be ridiculed as unattainable by some, but a goal that is consistent with the objective of supporting an ethical learning community. And it is a goal that, if not set, can never be achieved.

A love of academic integrity takes us beyond "gotcha" policing. A love of academic integrity will pull (not push) students into engagement with their learning assignments. While academic integrity policies and rules must be in place as a foundation for learning, it is our intention to articulate a higher vision to use rules only as a platform to promote a greater educational calling. That calling is to study, work, and learn together and achieve our best potential as mature thinkers in an ethical learning community. McCabe and Stephens (2006) write, "The goal should be to help students understand the importance of scholarship, intellectual property and integrity and to develop the will and skill to live life in a fair, honest and responsible manner." Developing the "will and skill" together is the objective of the following narrative. And in agreement with Scanlon (2003), we believe teachers should be educators of the process and not just policing their students.

This chapter will focus specifically on a definition of plagiarism as one aspect of dishonesty. It will provide examples of various forms of plagiarism and student justifications for plagiarism, arguments to resist these justifications, and a series of teacher strategies to help students avoid the act of plagiarism. It is hoped that the reader will cultivate both the will of the student to choose a life of academic integrity and the skill to practice integrity.

The Problem

Schab (1991) highlights the trends in high school student attitudes gathered in his research from 1969 to 1989 that notes the decrease in the perception that cheating is wrong. In our own current research (Stephens and Wangaard 2010), we have found that over 95 percent of students (sample size: 3,625) from a diverse selection of New England public high schools engaged in some form of academic dishonesty over the course of a recent school year. When questioned specifically about plagiarism, 47 percent to 66 percent (the range of percentages reported as the averages from six schools) reported copying a few sentences that they used in reports without citation (Stephens and Wangaard 2010).

These recent data only validate the historical trends highlighted by Schab and affirmed by McCabe and Stephens (2006), who note that one-quarter to one-third of undergraduate students report uncited cutting and pasting within their college writing. McCabe and Stephens state, "We believe Internet plagiarism, and cheating more broadly defined, is largely a symptom of a greater malaise affecting our culture—a shift in educational and ethical values that has transpired over the past several decades (e.g., Callahan 2004[a])." They go on to say that students may be confused by "abstract concepts such as intellectual property and copyright," and cite "the failure of many schools to adequately orient students on issues of academic integrity" and "administrators who fail to strongly support campus integrity policies" (McCabe and Stephens 2006).

One complicating factor in addressing plagiarism effectively is that many teachers and college faculty members do not necessarily agree on plagiarism when they see it. In one study of college professors, the investigators found that professors could not agree on the degree of plagiarism in six versions of rewrites from a journal article (Roig 2001). If college professors cannot clearly agree on examination of the same evidence, are our secondary teachers and students any better prepared to deal with the topic?

Defining Plagiarism

When discussing plagiarism, you often hear people euphemistically refer to an activity of borrowing or using the words, ideas, or products of others. This is a strategy of deflecting any ethical light that might be shed on the real behavior demonstrated, which is theft and fraud. In fact, *Merriam-Webster's Collegiate Dictionary*, 11th edition, gives the Latin root of "plagiarist" as *plagiarius*, "kidnapper." Kidnapping provides a descriptive image of someone using deception to take away and hold a person against her or his will. In human kidnapping, the victim will be greatly missed when the kidnapping is discovered. We all recognize that kidnap victims and their loved ones experience an intense sense of loss.

Can the metaphor of "kidnapping" words, ideas, images, or music communicate the same sense of loss to those victimized in the crime? Victims of plagiarism are certainly the legal owners of the original content along with those who are taken in by the fraud or theft. While the emotional attachment to ideas, products, and words will be less than an attachment to a person, the plagiarism of any product is still theft and fraud and should be clearly identified as such in support of an ethical learning community. Thus, a first step in resisting plagiarism is defining it with words that clearly identify the ethical problems associated with this behavior.

While it is rare to see criminal codes that resist plagiarism (US Legal Inc. 2008), there are legal restrictions (U.S. Copyright Office 2008) that protect intellectual property from unapproved use, whether cited or not. It is acknowledged that copyright and plagiarism are two different issues. One could accurately quote and provide citation and still violate copyright laws. Guidelines that provide some boundaries for fair use generally include works of criticism, comment, news reporting, teaching, scholarship, and research (U.S. Copyright Office 2009). To avoid copyright issues, it is always better to obtain permission to use copyrighted material.

Plagiarism alone has an extensive record in civil lawsuits and, of course, in the sanctions and discipline applied to students in schools. While most schools have their own policies that define plagiarism, the U.S. Office of Science and Technology Policy defines plagiarism as "the appropriation of another person's ideas, processes, results, or words without giving appropriate credit" (U.S. Office of Science and Technology 2000). This authoritative source certainly covers the domain of plagiarism; however, in an effort to avoid euphemisms, we prefer the definition cited by Lathrop and Foss (2000, as based on *Webster's Third New International Dictionary of the English Language*, unabridged): "Plagiarize: to steal and pass off as one's own (the ideas or words of another); use (a created production) without crediting the source; to commit literary theft; present as new and original an idea or product derived from an existing source" (p. 116). This second definition clearly identifies the theft and fraud that take place with plagiarism.

The Wrong Option: A Student's Story

I am a second year student in the Chemistry program. I plagiarized in five lab reports for a second year chemistry course during the Fall 2008 semester. My schedule was really bad [and] I barely had time to sit and spend time on lab reports. Before the semester started, some friend of mine gave me electronic copies for some old lab reports of his friend to help me out with the structure for writing out the lab reports. My friend warned me about copying the reports, telling me that I would easily get caught doing it, but I did not take his advice.

I was put in a situation where I had no time to do some of the assigned work. I had two options: the first option was to get a bad mark or a zero if I did not hand in the lab report. The second option, which seemed to be the faster and quickest option, was to plagiarize the lab reports given to me and hand them in as my own work. I chose the second option not thinking of the consequences that might occur if I got caught plagiarizing.

I never expected to be caught since the T.A. did not notice me plagiarizing in the first two labs. At the end of the semester I ended up with a grade of F in the course and received a four-month suspension. I have learned a big lesson from this experience, which is not to copy others' work and hand it in as my own work, because it is not fair for the person who spent time on it. I should think before I act from now on. My action was unethical . . . (Chemistry student 2009)

What Plagiarism Looks Like

There are multiple ways students can choose to plagiarize. Table 8.1 provides a synthesis of behaviors cited by multiple sources and gives a reasonable overview of behaviors that meet criteria for academic theft and fraud. While students often object to the accusation of plagiarism when they reuse their own work, most academic institutions that grant credit for projects want to see original work to grant new credit, or a citation when the author is including previous work in a new assignment.

Identifying and defining the various forms of plagiarism such as those in Table 8.1 are important steps for both teachers and students. It is recognized that teachers disagree about what constitutes plagiarism in various forms of paraphrasing without citation. It is important for educators to develop their own rubric to define acceptable practices for techniques like paraphrasing and citation and teach each other and their students these practices. Ideas for this will be presented in upcoming sections. It is also helpful for teachers to develop a clear awareness of typical plagiarism strategies and create assignments to resist these practices. It is important to inform students that teachers are aware of plagiarism techniques and are taking steps to counteract them while helping students achieve real learning through research, outlining, analysis, and their own writing. Clearly identifying plagiarism strategies as theft and fraud will also help resist the justifications that students often use when confronted with acts of plagiarism.

Why I Did It

Most people want to distance themselves from any allegation of theft and fraud. Thus, it is easy to understand how we use justifications or rationalizations to separate ourselves from behaviors we know to be wrong. A "good" justification will help me avoid taking responsibility for theft or fraud and allow me a psychological back door to keep my reputation clear in my own mind. One type of justification for cheating has been observed in students who perceive their teachers as unfair or uncaring (Stephens 2005).

In our recent study of six public high schools, the top three justifications cited by students for their participation in any cheating behaviors were academic pressure and stress on grades; time pressure; and (equal number of responses) poor teaching and not interested in subject (Stephens and Wangaard 2010).

Table 8.1. Forms of plagiarism

Plagiarism without Citation	Description
Copied or purchased	Whole document and claiming authorship
Cut and paste	Parts of single source copied word for word
Cut and paste patchwork	Parts of multiple sources copied word for word
Copied outline of document	Duplicating the outline and ideas of a whole document while changing the wording
Paraphrasing	Changing the wording of a short passage but communicating the original author's idea
Use of own previous work	Copying your own previous writing word for word
Editing/revisions by others	Major rewriting or revision of your work by others
Plagiarism with Citation	
Copied or cut and paste	Word-for-word copying with citation but without the use of quotations
Citations in text	Citations are included in text but not in bibliography
Inflated bibliography	Real bibliography references are provided but not cited in text
Phony bibliography	Bibliography references are made up
Insufficient citation	Information missing from citation or bibliography that prevents reader from finding reference

Sources: DeSena 2007; Gilmore 2008; Plagiarism dot Org 2009; Princeton University 2008; Whitley and Keith-Spiegel 2002.

Table 8.2. Rationalizations for academic dishonesty sorted by external and internal focus of control

Rationalizations for Academic Dishonesty with Primarily an External Focus	Rationalizations for Academic Dishonesty That Include Internal Focus
Grade pressure (to avoid failure or maintain high GPA)	Lack of ethical norms
Achievement pressure (parents, class rank, scholarship, future employment)	Self-doubt regarding abilities
Excessive academic workload and time pressure for schoolwork	Confused about standards
Others cheating, dishonesty is norm in cheating culture	Easy way out
Teachers don't hold students accountable; few cheaters get caught; no meaningful punishment	Disdain for assignment
Unfair instructor who doesn't teach well (grading too hard, tests unfair); excessive expectations	Disengaged from teacher
Other loyalties (helping a friend)	Minimizing seriousness, selective morality (only cheat on hard classes; it was only busywork; it was only one assignment; we were collaborating)
Irresistible opportunity: other students don't cover their papers; instructor left the room; found the exam	Denial of injury (no one is hurt)
Nonacademic time pressure; illness; job requirements; extracurricular activities; family	Poor time management and study skills; procrastination
	Lack of effort (didn't attend class, did not want to do work); not interested
	Enjoy the challenge of cheating

Sources: Gilmore 2008; Lathrop and Foss 2005; Strom and Strom 2005; Whitley and Keith-Spiegel 2002.

Clearly understanding and identifying these rationalizations can help teachers and students resist the temptation to use them in support of academic dishonesty in general and plagiarism specifically. In chapter 7, there is a worksheet titled "Integrity Neutralizers" (pages 141–142) that can support a class or advisor-advisee discussion about how students can create their own responses to refute rationalizations. Students' ability to identify and refute neutralizers is an important judgment and behavioral skill that can help them resist acts of plagiarism.

Reasons to Resist

It may seem obvious beyond the need to make the argument; in the present culture, however, we believe the argument needs to be clear. Why should we resist cheating and plagiarism? Table 8.3 provides a synthesis and analysis of reasons to resist plagiarism as cited in recent literature.

There are three major domains of concern as they relate to plagiarism that should motivate teachers, school leaders, and students themselves to resist plagiarism. Authentic learning and higher-order thinking is certainly challenged when students practice plagiarism. Some might argue that well-done cut-and-paste plagiarism does show that the student can comprehend and synthesize information into a new narrative, but that viewpoint negates the need for the student to do her or his own writing and ignores the issues of theft and fraud. Authentic learning and improvement in writing should demand that the student practice real analysis, synthesis, and evaluation with her or his own words and cite authors whose work has been quoted, referred to, or paraphrased.

Focusing on the student, one can identify several reasons plagiarism should be resisted. If we accept our definition that plagiarism is theft and fraud, then there is a corrosion of the student's character when he or she plagiarizes. While no one is suggesting a causal link to future moral indiscretions, there are correlations between plagiarism and other ethical lapses whereby researchers hypothesize that if one link is broken (plagiarism is resisted), it may help avoid the ethical corrosion of other antisocial behaviors (Lovett-Hooper et al. 2007; Whitley and Keith-Spiegel 2002).

Finally, there is a societal reason to resist plagiarism to protect the integrity among colleagues and students to teachers. The act of fraud and theft in academic settings can undermine the morale of all participants and is certainly recognized to give the cheater an advantage in gaining academic awards and promotions in addition to taking incentive away from those who work creatively for their own income when others can take it without attribution or fee.

Table 8.3. Reasons to resist plagiarism

Academic	• To protect authentic learning • To encourage student understanding, analysis, synthesis, critique with higher-order thinking skills through writing with their own words • Improved writing skills
Personal	• Pride in own work • Protecting your own integrity and character for yourself (reputation) and society • Avoiding the consequences of being caught • To discourage other antisocial behaviors that can be correlated to plagiarism
Others	• Respect for colleagues (you are not a fraud and you are not stealing from them) • Avoid theft and fraudulent behavior that gives you an advantage over others and deceives instructors • Protect student and faculty morale by maintaining authentic learning

Sources: DeSena 2007; Gilmore 2008; Lovett-Hooper et al. 2007; Menager-Beeley and Paulos 2006; Standler 2000; Stern 2007; Whitley and Keith-Spiegel 2002.

With the strength of these reasons to resist plagiarism, we turn now to strategies teachers can use to help students avoid this behavior.

Strategies to Help Avoid Plagiarism

Scheduling

Time pressure is often cited by students as the critical factor that led them to plagiarize. Students and their teachers can share a responsibility to schedule writing projects to help avoid this dilemma. While high school teachers might argue that their students are old enough to do their own scheduling, this reasoning misses the reality of school life where many students have not developed the skill. Thus, it is recommended that teachers create a schedule with mini-deadlines for any meaningful writing assignment. Scheduling deadlines can include the following:

- Topic selection and thesis statement
- Bibliography and notes
- Writing outline
- Writing draft
- Peer editing
- Final draft

This type of scheduling can serve three purposes. First, students are guided to meet these mini-deadlines, which help them learn successful scheduling skills and help reduce the temptation to plagiarize due to procrastination and time constraints. Two, there is a greater opportunity for genuine learning to take place as the students are responsible for demonstrating they have authentically worked on the essential components of the writing assignment that include researching, outlining, and drafting. And finally, scheduling appropriately divides and assigns a grade to the meaningful components of the assignment to reasonably balance the academic weight of each component. With this type of mini-deadline grading, students learn the value (as measured by a grade) of each component of the writing process.

A separate scheduling issue is uniquely a teacher/faculty responsibility. Given the availability of a variety of electronic scheduling devices such as Google Calendar, there is every reason to suggest that school faculty can internally monitor and balance the number of major assignments students in similar tracks will be expected to complete in a specific time period. Even large universities attempt to spread out final exam schedules according to block scheduling by academic disciplines. High schools could accomplish similar schedule segregation with some simple administrative communication. It is surprising how many teachers indicate they have no expectation of scheduling their major projects in collaboration with colleagues, but this step of respect for the students can help reduce some of the time pressure issues that create rationalizations for plagiarism.

Careful Note Taking from a Meaningful Literature Search

We have highlighted the idea of creating a mini-deadline and grade for researching a bibliography and note taking. In the era of the Internet, it can be daunting to demand resources that might not be found electronically. Depending on the topic and assignment, teachers need to be clear about their requirements for how a bibliography is formed. How many printed sources are required? How many secondary sources (electronic or printed) are acceptable? What citation standard is required?

Once the assignment is clarified, the real work of finding relevant and reliable sources and note taking begins. And this is real work that students often find to be challenging. Some students might complain, "I can just read the sources, complete my bibliography, and write the paper. Why do you insist on seeing my notes?" This argument might be accurate for the rare and gifted student, but even gifted students can profit from the step of note taking. If done properly, note taking can help students avoid the pitfalls of plagiarism and also promote meaningful analysis and synthesis of sources for their own writing.

Proper note taking—whether done with electronic tools like Endnote or with some form of word processing software, or completed with a pen and index cards—requires students first and foremost to capture the full citation of a reference and always make sure to identify quotes with a page number. Note taking without these two requirements will fail the student in her or his attempt to cite properly or avoid the use of quotes without proper attribution. Thus, it must be a clear expectation that all quotations recorded in notes are in quotation marks, or if captured electronically, the quotes are in italics and set within indented margins.

Citation methods will be addressed shortly, but the important key here is to have a clear citation requirement such as national standards from the American Psychology Association (APA) or Modern Language Association (MLA) and provide students with tools and examples to put these citation strategies into practice. It is best for students if the school faculty can agree upon one format to practice within a school district; however, we recognize there are always situations where students might be called upon to use a standard different from the school's and they should know how to find resources to meet those expectations.

The full citation should always be completed first with whatever means the student is taking their notes. With a completed citation, the student then can begin to learn the skill of note taking. We recommend that teachers teach and practice note taking strategies with their students. Using one passage from a shared text, have students practice finding and writing out the main point, a quote that would effectively communicate the main point and provide supporting facts for the main point. Have students peer-review their classmates' notes to compare and discuss their observations. In class, have students share their observations and record on a flip chart or SMART Board the observations shared by classmates. The skill of note taking needs to be taught and practiced as an essential strategy to help students avoid plagiarism. A thoughtful scope and sequence will include developmentally appropriate teaching objectives for students to gain mastery in the skill of note taking over their school career.

Most note taking should simply involve recording facts, ideas, or quotes from the source being cited; however, we recognize that during note taking students will have their own ideas or questions develop. Recording personal thoughts and questions within the note taking exercise can ultimately be helpful in creating the outline and then writing the draft paper. Care should be taken to encourage students to clearly identify where their thoughts and questions are recorded and where the cited author(s)' points are being recorded. There are a variety of ways to segregate this type of work. The software product Endnote allows a student to capture narrative in a "Notes" section as opposed to an "Abstract" section. Other methods can be suggested such as putting all personal reflections inside of brackets with their own initials: "[my thoughts . . . DBW]."

Finally, Princeton University's Academic Integrity guidelines encourage their students to keep all of their raw notes and save them electronically (Princeton University 2008). The goal is to provide a record of comparison to the final paper if a charge of academic dishonesty is ever raised. In addition to protection during any inquiry into plagiarism, careful note taking will also provide a tremendous resource for the next strategy of writing to avoid plagiarism, namely, the development of a detailed outline.

Outlining

Developing an effective outline can serve students in two important ways. First, this is the time for students to practice their higher-order thinking skills to take the knowledge they have gained in their research and note taking and demonstrate comprehension of the subject matter by completing an analysis of various ideas, making their own synthesis or evaluating someone else's work or ideas. This is real academic work that is short-circuited if the students do not create their own outlines and instead copy and paste the thinking of others. Failing to develop their own outlines robs the students of a learning opportunity and increases the pressure to steal the work of others, which defrauds the teacher and their peers.

The second benefit of effective outlining is to create a logical flow for the narrative that is to be written. The student's thesis statement can be edited for the outline and the supporting points, and details can be organized to support the thesis and ultimately the conclusion. Quotes can be identified that uniquely support a point in the narrative. Anecdotes or stories that would support the narrative can be integrated into an outline. Connecting vocabulary can be identified that will link the flow of the narrative. Students with detailed outlines should rarely have the issue of writer's block as they can be encouraged just to keep working to fill in the details of their outline from their own research.

Outlining is another skill set that must be taught and practiced in class to encourage student success. As with note taking, practice can be accomplished in class by taking shared experiences or stories and having the students develop their own outline to retell the story. Identifying main points, properly ordering supporting facts, and highlighting useful quotes or anecdotes for placement in an outline can be useful study and writing strategies. As the skill of outlining is developed, students will experience less pressure to cut and paste someone else's writing to create their own narrative.

The specific mechanics of outlining, such as the use of numbers or letters and their indentations, will take us beyond the detail we intend to cover in this toolkit. A variety of methods exist that are supported by most word processing programs, and as with the methods of citation, they should be established as a standard for a school district. Beyond the specific mechanics, the goal is to help the students think, analyze, organize, and have a detailed outline to complete their writing well.

Quoting

Misquotations are the only quotations that are never misquoted.

Hesketh Pearson

Quotations can be effectively used to highlight points or emphasize concepts that are exceptionally well stated by the original author. There are a number of commonly understood rules that apply in the use of quotes (Menager-Beeley and Paulos 2006; Stern 2007), and several are noted here:

- Use quotes in moderation and encourage students to use their own voice whenever possible.
- Do not change any of the vocabulary or punctuation within the quote.
- If quotes exceed four lines of text, place the quote in block indentation (10 spaces on left and right margin) and drop the quotation marks.
- Use three period marks to indicate that words have been deleted from a quote.
- Place brackets around any words that have been added to quotes to connect the narrative.
- Indicate the recognition of a grammar or spelling error in a quote with the word *sic* placed in brackets.
- Always note the page number in parentheses at the end of a quote.

Helping students to identify effective quotes and discussing the merit of certain quotes is another excellent classroom activity. This skill set can be practiced in class with the two goals of preparing students to identify and properly cite quotes in their own narratives.

Paraphrasing and Summarizing

Understanding why, when, and how to paraphrase is a meaningful writing skill for students, and paraphrasing always requires a citation. Well-done paraphrasing is accomplished when students are able to restate information or an idea in their own words, using their own sentence structure, while not changing the meaning or intention of the original author (Menager-Beeley and Paulos 2006).

Several goals can be accomplished when students paraphrase well. Students demonstrate their own understanding of the material as they are able to restate it in their own voice. In addition, students' narrative flow and style are not interrupted with a quote. And as noted by Stern (2007), paraphrasing provides the student an opportunity to restate in language that might be more readable for a new audience such as recasting language from a technical journal into narrative that a student's peers can understand.

Barry Gilmore, in his excellent 2008 book *Plagiarism: Why It Happens and*

How to Prevent It, provides a number of exercises for teachers to help students practice the skill of paraphrasing. Some of those resources are also available through his website at barrygilmore.weebly.com. Students need to be taught to think about and practice the skill of paraphrasing. It is a great strategy to help develop student comprehension of written material and provides the foundation for describing the work of other authors while setting the student up to compare, contrast, and summarize ideas in their own narrative.

Summarizing is a similar process to paraphrasing, but with the added goal of reducing the length of the narrative created by the original author. Summarizing, like paraphrasing, also requires a citation. We provide an example here using text from Horacek (2009) with a theme relevant to this chapter.

Narrative to be summarized:

The goal is ultimately to awaken a realization that the full codes of academic integrity are necessary for research to be possible, and that every serious research endeavor presupposes the good faith and sincerity of each participant. Ironically, published policies on academic integrity may hinder the appreciation of this point, since they present integrity too narrowly. Policies tell students not to cheat, plagiarize, or falsify data. What students need to know is that we expect them to aim far higher: their aim should be to get it right. Students reach intellectual adulthood when they feel a personal obligation to get it right in their work—and when the importance of getting it right contributes to the motivation for their effort. If we contrast these motivations with those of students who aim merely at abiding by the rules and getting good grades, the difference between them is this: the former have internalized the codes of academic integrity. They grasp that these are the very glue that binds an inquiring community, and they are thinking for themselves as members of that community. They have passed the transition point at which they realize that they are responsible—and should be held responsible—for the ideas they present as their own. If this is our aim, as I think it should be, we have not adequately addressed the issue of academic integrity when we have merely explained "the rules" and found strategies to enforce them vigilantly. (Horacek 2009, p. 16)

Example of summarized narrative:

Academic integrity policies and enforcing those policies fall short of Horack's (2009) desire to help students become intrinsically motivated to "get it right" (p. 16) and become members of an academic community with a sense of responsibility and personal obligation to think for themselves.

Students may then use summarized texts with proper citations to compare and analyze the ideas of multiple authors or to compare another author's main points to their own ideas. This is an important step in creating narratives where the students can complete the presentation of their own analysis, synthesis, or evaluation. All the skills of the writing process are the scaffolding that holds up students as they build their narratives. Without the skill development to appropriately schedule, identify, and cite a useful bibliography, take effective notes, create a detailed outline, understand how to use quotes, paraphrase, and summarize, students can fall into another category of rationalization to plagiarize by claiming an inability to complete the work.

Proper Citation

We have already noted the importance of teaching students proper citation methods as they research their literature resources (electronic or in print) and record notes from their sources. It is incumbent on the teacher to clearly describe the citation methodology that is required (hopefully a uniform policy throughout the school) and provide examples of typical citations for books, online resources, journals, etc. If a nationally recognized citation format is used, such as MLA, there are a variety of online resources that can provide ready assistance to students. One free example for MLA writing rules can be found at Capitol Community College's (Hartford, Connecticut) *Guide to Writing Research Papers* at www.ccc.commnet.edu/mla/practical_guide.shtml. For more scholarly writing, students should always be encouraged to purchase the software or published handbooks for the particular citation format they are required to use.

Without attempting to duplicate examples of citation that can be found in other texts or online, there are a few questions that teachers should address as they establish their citation criteria. Some of these questions are as follows:

- What citation format is required—APA, MLA, other?
- How are citations to be presented—bibliography or list of works cited with parenthetical references in text, footnotes, endnotes?
- Where can examples be found for in-text citation and the bibliography? Include examples of authors citing other sources.
- How many references are required for the bibliography or how many references need to be cited? Clearly identify the type of references required and specify the expectation for print or online references.

These basic questions can be addressed in an assignment outline that could also include the details of assignment components with mini-deadlines and grade weighting for each component. All this information is designed to clearly communicate expectations and information to help students avoid the snare of plagiarism either from time pressure or a lack of understanding the requirements.

Editing

There are several editing strategies that teachers may consider as students complete their drafts, including online editing services, peer editing, outside reviewers, and, obviously, the teacher's own review and comments. If your school has purchased the services of a commercial editing tool such as Turnitin.com, students may electronically submit their draft papers and receive a comprehensive report on the originality of their work based on a comparison to Turnitin's database. While there are stories of students learning to fool some electronic evaluations, the technology affords a very useful device in an age when so much material is available to students online. Teachers need to address their own philosophical concerns regarding the use of such electronic services, but as a formative editing device, there is great review and reporting power available to the students and teacher.

Peer editing provides another firewall, albeit a possibly thin wall, to resist plagiarism. If the teacher constructs a meaningful editing rubric, the students' peers can be held accountable for their peer review steps to ascertain the student authors' understanding of their papers and the authenticity of their bibliographies compared to the research notes. There is an example of a peer editing form in chapter 7 (the Integrity Essay Grading Rubric, pages 126–127). While this form does not emphasize the investigation of original writing, it does provide an example of a detailed editing form that can be used by students during peer editing.

The Assignment

Teaching and having students practice the research and writing skills described in this chapter will go a long way in combating plagiarism. The final recommendation here is to evaluate the assignment itself and how it is designed and presented as one more strategy for promoting academic integrity. An assignment sheet with all the specific assignment components, deadlines, and expectations should include the teacher's own statement about the importance of practicing academic integrity and penalties (see chapter 4, page 68, for example penalties) if students are found to have plagiarized. In addition, how the assignment is designed can make plagiarism an easy or almost impossible task.

Teachers who design assignments to solicit higher-order thinking from students can integrate specific tasks of analysis that require students to think and bring into their writing their own reflection about experiences or other readings that would not be available from a cut-and-paste resource online (DeSena 2007). For example, let us compare two assignments related to Harper Lee's 1960 novel *To Kill a Mockingbird*:

Assignment One

Describe and analyze the ethical character of Atticus Finch in the novel *To Kill a Mockingbird* and cite at least three examples from the novel for your analysis.

Assignment Two

Describe and analyze the ethical character of Atticus Finch in the novel *To Kill a Mockingbird* and cite at least three examples from the novel for your analysis.

Compare your analysis of Atticus Finch to choices demonstrated by _____ in [reference to recent newspaper or magazine article] (attached)

Evaluate the ethical character of Atticus Finch and support or refute with at least two clear points the statement, "Atticus Finch's ethics would help me to personally live a meaningful and productive life."

Assignment One is written with the expectation that the student would read the novel and be able to practice some higher-order thinking to identify and analyze the ethical character of Atticus Finch in the novel *To Kill a Mockingbird*. This is a reasonable assignment and could support meaningful thinking, writing, and discussion in class. Assignment One could also be easily plagiarized by a student searching for similar essays completed and published on the Internet.

Assignment Two begins with the same premise to comprehend and analyze the ethical character of Mr. Finch, and goes on to add the requirement of comparing this analysis to some event or person (as determined by the teacher's selection of a recently published story) and the additional personal application of the analysis and evaluation. The extra requirements make the possibility of plagiarizing the whole assignment almost impossible. The student must make some comparison to a recent event and ultimately make application to him- or herself. No one would have previously published anything close to this assignment on the Internet. The student is compelled to think, analyze, and write.

The simple comparison presented here can be extended to almost any subject matter where the lessons completed in most U.S. high schools can be modified to compare, analyze, and evaluate in light of another author, current event, or personal application. It is the teachers' creativity that will enhance the relevance of the lesson to the student, extend the opportunity for the student to practice good thinking, and create a meaningful deterrent to plagiarism.

An additional strategy that would impede the plagiarist would include the requirement of some form of meta-analysis at the end of an assignment and presented as an oral report (Lathrop and Foss 2000). Students who recognize that some form of oral summary will be required at the end of the assignment will also understand that their own comprehension of the material will be tested during this presentation. An assignment that requires students to present their analysis and evaluation orally will demand that students be able to clearly articulate the points they make in their written narrative. A plagiarized narrative will be much harder for students to defend.

Finally, if the school has an honor code, this is a good time for the teacher to have students reflect upon that code on the printed assignment sheet or with the students' own affirmation on the assignments they turn in. Gilmore (2008) suggests the following pledge to be written and signed by the student: "I pledge on my honor that this paper represents my own work" (p. 131). Other examples of school and work pledges can be found in chapter 3, pages 57–58.

Teachable Moment

Enforcing academic integrity policies can be a teachable moment for more than just students. A now infamous story about policy enforcement occurred in 2002 at Piper High School, a small Kansas school 20 miles west of Kansas City (see Wilgoren 2002).

A sophomore biology class was annually assigned a semester-long project that included a contract signed by students and parents stipulating the consequence of a zero grade for plagiarism. The teacher grew concerned when evidence of plagiarism became evident during a review of project drafts. The biology teacher alerted students of her concerns and reminded them of the consequences in her feedback on the project drafts.[1] Many students chose to ignore the warnings.

When the final projects were submitted, Internet searches confirmed that 28 of 118 students plagiarized text in their final draft. With the principal's support, the teacher assigned a zero for the project, which led to many failing grades for the semester.

Some parents were outraged and petitioned the principal, who continued his support for the teacher. A group of parents took their concern to the school board. The board heard the case and overruled the teacher and principal. The board mandated that the teacher lower the percentage of assignment weight in the semester grade and lower the percentage penalty for plagiarism in the assignment. This action allowed students who had plagiarized to earn a passing grade for the semester and lowered the semester grades of some students who had not plagiarized on the project and had earned a high grade.

On returning to school the day after the board meeting, some students mocked the biology teacher in her class. Multiple other anecdotes of reactions in and out of the community were noted: Piper students were publically challenged not to cheat during regional SAT testing; Kansas State

University deans wrote a letter to the school board cautioning them that Piper students must respect the university's honor code; posters mocking Piper students as cheaters showed up at athletic events at other schools; and parents challenged the decision at a follow-up board meeting. The biology teacher resigned the day after the board meeting, and ultimately the principal, vice-principal, and nine of 31 faculty left the district that spring (*People* 2002).

Some parents of students who plagiarized felt the biology teacher had missed a teachable moment to instruct the students rather than discipline them. Others voiced support for the teacher and maintained that the discipline was a teachable moment in itself. Clearly this incident was a teachable moment for all involved and provides a lesson today as to the need to be clear and consistent with students and parents in the policies that support school academic integrity.

Wrapping Up Plagiarism

Our goal with this chapter has been to outline steps that can be taken to resist plagiarism and promote the development of an ethical learning community. Any policies, writing skills, and teacher strategies are secondary to the clear objective of promoting academic integrity as a core value of the students and faculty. While this is a challenging aspiration, individual teachers can play an important role in the task even in the absence of school-wide support. Students will perceive and respect teachers who are invested in their students and demonstrate authentic support of core values such as integrity. Much research has shown the positive correlation between students' avoidance of cheating and respect for their teacher (Stephens 2005).

NOTE

1. M. Adams (October 20, 2005), personal communication at Center for Academic Integrity Conference, Virginia Tech University, Blacksburg, VA.

Case Studies of Cultural Change

Introduction to Project Case Studies

In 2007, the School for Ethical Education (SEE), in collaboration with the University of Connecticut (UCONN) Neag School of Education, received a grant[1] to develop, implement, and evaluate a three-year intervention project. The primary goal of the project was to promote academic integrity and reduce cheating and plagiarism among high school students. A total of six high schools were recruited to participate in the project: three as participating or "pilot" schools and three as nonparticipating or "control" schools. All six were public schools in the northeastern United States: two served predominantly lower-middle-class communities with approximately 50 percent minority populations; two schools served predominantly upper-middle-income communities with predominately White students; and two schools served higher-income communities.

The administration of each project pilot school agreed to form an Academic Integrity Committee to include administration, faculty, and students. The AICs' mission was to develop, implement, and evaluate a two-year strategic plan promoting academic integrity using the conceptual model described in chapter 1. Thus, the formation of a well-functioning AIC was the centerpiece of the intervention strategy employed in this project. Details concerning the composition, establishment, and key activities of these AICs are discussed in chapter 2. In this appendix, we offer case study narratives of the three pilot schools and one of the control schools (which agreed to participate as a control school if it could become a pilot school in year two of the project). Each case offers a unique insight into the promises, possibilities, and pitfalls associated with undertaking a school-wide intervention project.

Bronze High School: A Case of Perseverance

Bronze High School is situated in a mature and diverse suburban community that is adjacent to a medium-sized New England city. The student population exceeded 1,500 and is almost 50 percent minority, with the largest segment of the minority population being African American. Approximately 35 percent of the students qualified for free and reduced lunch subsidies.

AIC Composition and Dynamics

The Bronze AIC formed solidly in its first year around a core group of students, and several underclassman girls became officers in the fall of the second year. The students worked collaboratively with the regular support of four to five faculty members representing different disciplines within the school. One faculty person, who was also a department chair, took the lead sponsorship role throughout the study. AIC meetings were hosted regularly and often on a biweekly basis with an average attendance of about 14 students and two to three faculty members. One parent attended two or three meetings. Student attendance varied with one or two meetings having only two to three students and other meetings attracting as many as 40 students. Students and faculty always appreciated the provision of pizza and sodas, and the food seemed to encourage initial meeting attendance. During the third school year, AIC members participated in 21 different meetings or events, not including any preparation activities in between meetings and events. In year three, the sponsor also had a student officer volunteer two to three periods each week to support AIC project administration.

The AIC kept making progress because of the consistency of the adult sponsors and student leaders who took genuine ownership of their work and that of the group. Students chose leadership roles early in the second year, and this, along with the successful administration of the school's pledge drive (with AIC members wearing AIC T-shirts), seemed to galvanize the group with an identity and sense of accomplishment. There had been much foundational work completed in the previous spring (see accomplishments noted below), but the completion of the school academic integrity pledge drive was the AIC's coming-out event.

Unique Circumstances

The strategic planning process completed by the Bronze school's AIC documented a variety of student and faculty concerns, which included an awareness that past school-wide initiatives had been started but not followed up with sufficient energy to make a difference, and that a level of cynicism may exist that could undermine any attempt to alter the school culture. These faculty members and students expressed skepticism that real progress could be made to advance academic integrity even though the need was great. Subsequent survey work confirmed the need to address academic integrity issues at the student and faculty level. The principal changed at the end of year two; however, the new principal seemed to take a genuine interest in the success of the project. Regardless of the administration change, student and faculty dedication to the AIC mission kept the group on track to accomplish a remarkable number of tasks.

Accomplishments

One needs to pause to consider what each one of the following accomplishments means in terms of time, preparation, and follow-up. The Bronze AIC can certainly be commended for completing or implementing these initiatives:

- Complete strategic assessment and drafted goals for strategic plan
- AIC narratives that include AIC mission, code of conduct, information flyer, motto, logo
- Statement with new school honor code approved by the faculty and posted in all classrooms
- Publication of honor pledge and administration of pledge drive, which provided students with integrity bracelets and pledge cards if they would recite and sign the pledge
- Design and purchase of AIC T-shirts for AIC members to wear during AIC activities
- Establishment of AIC student leadership roles and renewal of roles for year four
- Administration of integrity essay-writing contest in years two and three
- Purchase and setup of AIC event tent at school-wide events (homecoming, first-year orientation) with pledge drive and AIC information
- Presentations at two faculty meetings
- Presentation at one district board meeting
- Creation of AIC website linked to school website
- Design and dissemination of two advisor-advisee lessons with academic integrity lessons
- Implementation of Integrity Word of the Week on school announcements in spring of year two
- Administration of an integrity movie night
- Administration of two outreach classes to all district elementary schools with integrity lessons
- AIC student officers and two sponsors participated in a panel presentation during a national conference in Washington, D.C., in year three
- Articles about the AIC were published in school and local papers in years two and three

- AIC drafted revision of school handbook policy on academic integrity in year three and which was approved by faculty and school board in year four.

Reflection

A researcher's journal entries made several observations regarding the classical issues associated with the administration of volunteer groups, including the following:

- The need for the AIC to attend to "social and teambuilding norms" such as having members know one another's names and sharing greetings or goodbyes at the start and end of meetings, acknowledging the suggestions of others, clearly identifying roles and duties for all participants, and following up on assignments;
- Establishing expectations for attendance and taking account of absences;
- Taking and publishing notes for attendance, meeting topics, and assignments; and
- Using the notes from the past meeting to establish a new meeting agenda and publishing the agenda.

These observations are all the little details that successful groups ultimately accomplish to become a team and achieve their goals. By the end of the third year, the Bronze AIC was addressing many of these issues to help them move forward as well as they did to improve the awareness of academic integrity in their school. In the administration of the third-year Academic Motivation and Integrity Survey (AMIS) survey, it was rare for students not to recognize that the AIC was functioning in their school.

Silver High School: A Case of the Importance of Commitment and Leadership

Located in an upper-middle-class suburban community approximately 30 minutes from the closest city center, Silver High School is a midsize school (about 1,200 students) serving a predominantly White student community. Only 10 percent of the students were from minority groups (with Asian Americans representing the largest subgroup), and less than 3 percent of the student population qualified for a free and reduced lunch subsidy. It is, like many schools with its demographic profile, a high-achieving school. For example, when asked about the academic climate at their school, over 80 percent of students responded either "mostly true" or "very true" to the statement, "In this school, grades and test scores are talked about a lot." Conversely, less than 45 percent of students responded similarly to the statement, "In this school, the emphasis is on really understanding schoolwork, not just memorizing it." Finally, it is a school where 98 percent plan on attending college (approximately 60 percent aspiring to earn an advanced degree), and nearly 50 percent agreed or strongly agreed with the statement, "It is all right to cheat when your future happiness or success is at stake."

In the lexicon of the renowned psychologist Martin Covington (1992), these students (and the broader community from which they come) are "over-strivers": highly oriented toward success but deeply anxious about not achieving success. As detailed below, this prevailing ethos manifested itself in a number of ways during our visits to the school during the first two years of the project, and it explains some of the struggles and shortcomings Silver High encountered as its AIC attempted to promote academic integrity.

AIC Composition and Dynamics

As with our other pilot schools, Silver High started off with a great deal of enthusiasm and quickly formed a solid AIC composed of student representatives from each grade level and six teachers from three different academic departments. During year two, the committee grew to include an administrator (a vice-principal) and a parent. As required, the AIC met biweekly during years one and two. While attendance and morale at these meetings were good, the meetings were always kept to an hour or less, and the time between meetings was not used to accomplish meaningful tasks.

It soon became clear that these meetings, and the project more generally, were not a priority at this school. The priority, clearly and unequivocally, was student academic achievement. As depicted in the introduction to this case, Silver High is a high-pressure environment. In both subtle and tangible ways, concern about student grades, test scores, and college admissions (to elite colleges) defines and dominates its cultural landscape. Such an ethos is not inherently wrong or bad, but becomes problematic when coupled with fear or anxiety about not "making the grade" (Covington 1992). It leaves little room or time for other activities and ultimately undermines the ones that manage to get started.

In relation to Silver High's participation in the *Achieving with Integrity* project, this erosion of commitment was manifest in several ways. As noted earlier, meetings were always short and very little (if anything at all) happened between them. Additionally, meeting agendas seemed to be created at the last minute and meeting minutes were rarely taken (or at least not shared with the researchers, despite repeated requests). Finally, and most importantly, there was no public action taken by the AIC. Whereas the two other project schools were creating and carrying out various types of campaigns to promote academic integrity, Silver High failed to do so (despite the offering of numerous suggestions and much encouragement by the authors of this toolkit). The reasons for this failure are myriad and complex, but largely lead back to the culture. Simply put, Silver High was too concerned with doing *well* to invest seriously in doing *good*.

Unique Circumstances

Silver High encountered a unique (in our project) challenge during its three-year involvement in the project: change in leadership. Such a challenge is not unique, or even rare, in K–12 education. However, it can be detrimental to the kind of school reform effort and culture change our project was designed to bring about. This is especially so if multiple changes occur over a short period of time: Silver High had two changes in principal over the course of the three years it was involved in the project. While the reason for the first change was clear and anticipated (retirement), the reason for the latter change was neither transparent nor expected. Regardless of the reasons, cycling through two principals in three years took its toll on the morale of the school's faculty. Many communicated a sense of uncertainty and anxiety about the situation, which at the time of writing this toolkit was still unresolved.

Accomplishments

As noted above, Silver High's AIC never created or carried out a public campaign to promote academic integrity within the student body. It did, however, achieve a significant accomplishment during year two. Specifically, the committee worked very hard on a revision of the school's definition of and policies related to academic integrity. The original policy—like so many in secondary and postsecondary schools—was vague in its articulation of the meaning and importance of integrity, as well as too simplistic and purely punitive in its response to academic dishonesty. Regarding academic dishonesty, there was no differentiation in punishment based on the severity of the offense—all offenses received the same half-day detention—and there was no effort to remediate the behavior through education. The new policy that the AIC drafted addressed both these typical shortcomings by making distinctions between cheating on homework and more serious offenses (i.e., plagiarism and cheating on tests), as well as mandating completion of a program (to be developed) designed to help students think about and learn from their mistake. The new policy was submitted to central administration, where, for reasons never fully explained to the researchers, it was not approved.

Reflection

As the subtitle of this case suggests, we offer this case as an example of the importance of both commitment and leadership. Both are instrumental to the success of long-term, cultural change projects such as this one.

Gold High School: A Case of Great Parent Support

Gold is a high-achieving school located in a suburban to rural community that includes a large number of very expensive residential properties. The student population of about 1,000 is over 90 percent White and the largest minority group is Asian Americans. Less than 1 percent of the student population qualified for a free and reduced lunch subsidy.

AIC Composition and Dynamics

The Gold AIC renamed itself the Achieving with Integrity Committee (AWIC) to expand its mission beyond just academic integrity. The AWIC began with a remarkable diversity of faculty (approximately 12 participants), parents, and a few students. The number of faculty representatives declined in year two, and by year three the AWIC averaged four to five faculty/administration members, three to five students, and three to four parents. The group established student and adult leadership roles at the end of year two, which carried over to year three and led to the election of new officers for year four. In year one, two underclassman girls were the most actively engaged and became AWIC officers. These two students provided consistent student leadership through their senior year. The parent volunteers were also remarkably engaged in all three years of the study and proved to be strategic supporters in projects that were implemented in year three.

Unique Circumstances

The adult sponsorship shifted from a school counselor to a teacher in year two. The teacher who assumed leadership in the second year had not been part of the original committee, and thus there were some gaps in communication that required extra effort to overcome. The school administration demonstrated a moderate level of interest in the study, but resisted scheduling the faculty professional development activity that was part of the project design and struggled to accommodate the administration of the AMIS survey. In the first administration of the AMIS survey, the faculty actually showed little support and failed to secure the necessary student participation to justify a sample size. There was open frustration expressed by the faculty that the survey would take up class time at the end of the year. The project survey protocol needed to be redesigned with a passive student permission form to accommodate the reluctance of this school faculty in a high-achieving school. In year three there were also concerns expressed about the implementation of the survey, but with our shared review of the original letter of agreement, the AWIC teacher sponsor was authorized to help secure the necessary classes to implement the survey. With the passive student approval process, the survey was successfully administered with some modest gaps as some classes had field trips on the scheduled survey day.

The faculty survey that was completed by the AWIC revealed a super majority of support for the continued implementation of academic integrity policies and a willingness to learn more about strategies to encourage integrity. The faculty survey did note a small number of faculty dissenters who expressed concern about the AWIC's mission. It is assumed that one member of this dissenting group helped motivate a student to object to an AWIC project in year three.

In year three, the AWIC's *You Got It: We Caught It* campaign was designed to recognize students who had demonstrated some form of integrity. Integrity was to be defined broadly.

The AWIC brainstormed a list of possible examples of integrity such as honesty in self-reporting mistakes in grading (not in student's favor), returning lost items, standing up for your opinion in the face of some adversity, providing evidence that the opportunity to cheat was resisted, and exemplary demonstrations of good sportsmanship. All of the behaviors to be recognized were positive actions, and none of the examples encouraged or sought students to report the academic dishonesty of others. The AWIC had recruited all faculty and staff to be observers with *Caught You* certificates that if a student's act of integrity was spotted, that would lead to the student's being entered into a raffle for gift certificate awards. The AWIC would also seek to use the student's story (if voluntarily provided) in a follow-up awareness campaign about integrity.

One student took exception to the use of extrinsic awards for students observed to be acting with integrity. The student wrote a critical, two-page open letter to the AWIC and published it on his Facebook account. He wrote in the defense of integrity as he assumed that integrity would be corrupted by the association of any extrinsic reward given to students to promote it. He also accused the AWIC of attempting to bribe students to turn in other students who were cheating to get an extrinsic award. There were other inaccuracies, which the author failed to check out with the AWIC before he published his letter, and all of it led to quite a lot of conversation in the school. Following the publication of this open letter, the AWIC's bulletin board was graffitied with more criticisms, which led to more buzz in the school about integrity.

The controversy regarding the *Caught You* campaign also led a faculty member to come to an AWIC meeting to express his own concerns about the AWIC's mission and strategies. At that meeting, it became clear to the AWIC members who was the catalyst for the student's publication of the open letter. The faculty member explained his concern for extrinsic awards and the possibility of students being rewarded for informing on classmates. It became very clear in the teacher's description of his concern, in his vocabulary, and in his misconceptions that he was the inspiration for the student's open letter. The faculty person also noted that the student writer was one of his advisor-advisee members and that the topic had been the focus of their last meeting.

This story points out a not-so-unique dynamic that took place when a change initiative was introduced within this high-performing school community. It is recognized that some faculty can easily take umbrage at new initiatives such as an AWIC and express their frustration without discussing it with the source of the concern. The popularity and power of an electronic social network's publication of these concerns created meaningful negative feedback in the school. Anyone familiar with school change initiatives recognizes this as behavior that is to be expected in schools. Academic Integrity Committees should be well warned that their honorable cause is not immune to dissent (merited or unmerited).

Another important observation about Gold High School is the active and consistent contribution by three to five parents. Three parents in particular were engaged from the founding of the AIC and were instrumental in some of the larger projects completed in year three. Their professional competence, patience with school process, and commitment to the mission were exemplary and unique among the study schools in support of AIC projects.

Accomplishments

The Gold AWIC completed an outstanding range of projects and narratives that included the following:

- AWIC strategic plan with multiple goals that guided efforts in year two
- AWIC mission, code of conduct, motto, and logo
- Revision of the school's honor code and creation of an honor pledge
- A poster contest
- A faculty survey
- AWIC presentations at faculty meetings in years two and three
- Initiated one advisor-advisee lesson focused on academic integrity
- Revision of student handbook statement regarding academic integrity
- First-year orientation in year three
- Establishment of AWIC student and adult officers
- Election of new officers for year four
- Template for meeting notes and task assignments
- Purchase of AWIC pop-up tent and large banner for public events
- Implementation of honor pledge campaign during school-wide spring open house with 102 student pledge signers in year two and repeated in year three
- Completion of AWIC video
- Administration of Integrity Week, which included "exam relief" goody bags with integrity messages on pencils, a stress ball, a water bottle, and other items
- Creation of award-winning integrity exemplar posters with quotes and pictures of students

- Administration of *Caught You* campaign recognizing acts of integrity
- AWIC story published in local newspaper
- Presentation of academic integrity assembly and pledge/membership drive in two local middle schools

Reflection

At the start of this integrity project, each pilot school was given a three-ring binder that provided resources and articles about academic integrity as well as strategies to organize and run AIC meetings. It is meaningful to note that the researchers sought to encourage the AIC leadership at Gold High School to use these resources without much effect in year one. The researcher's journal includes many references to failures to practice simple meeting procedures that would have helped the AIC get up and running. Procedures that would have supported team building (gaining name recognition, briefly sharing personal stories, assigning and following up on tasks) and procedures that would have facilitated more efficient progress (attendance expectation, recording and publishing notes with assigned tasks, following up on identified strategic goals) did not become the norm until after the change in leadership in year two. In all three years of the project there were challenges in gaining the participation of more students and consistently having faculty attend. The gaps in effective meeting organization may have been one reason faculty and students did not sustain their membership. Intermittent attendance by faculty and students was a frustration for the teacher sponsor and parents. Progress on the goal of regular attendance was made by the end of year three.

Two parents were actually the most consistent in attendance and follow-up on tasks. This parent engagement led several projects in year three that were all accomplished with excellence, the most noteworthy being the outreach to the two local middle schools as a result of parent contacts. Parents opened the door to a project where students organized and put on an assembly for the grade 8 students, which led to definitions of academic integrity, invitations to sign an honor pledge, and recruitment to join the AWIC when they came to high school in the fall. The entire project—including transportation, obtaining necessary permissions, and organization and implementation of the assembly—was an example of excellent student-adult collaboration and a terrific demonstration of the effectiveness of an AWIC.

It was through the completion of this middle school assembly project that the researcher believed that both the students and adults began to understand the full meaning of the project conceptual model and accept the following key points: (1) students, parents, and faculty recognized academic dishonesty as a moral issue and as something corrosive to schools and the individual, (2) students need to learn how to recognize and refute the rationalizations of cheating, and (3) students need to develop skill sets to help them choose to practice integrity when they recognize the temptation to cheat. All three of these points became central to the main message of the middle school assembly, and in the opinion of the researcher, this was the first time the AWIC as a group recognized all the arguments in support of the conceptual model guiding its mission. Thus, as opposed to simply resisting cheating (which all AWIC members would have acknowledged as a minimalist mission), the AWIC learned by teaching the grade 8 students the importance of developing ethical and moral awareness, moral judgment, moral commitment, and skills to act on their moral commitment.

Gold Control High School: A Case of Frustration

Gold Control was a control school for Gold High School and represented similar demographics, with over 90 percent of the students being White, and while it is modestly larger, with about 1,200 students, Gold Control had less than 1 percent on free and reduced lunch subsidy.

AIC Composition and Dynamics

As they were recruited to this integrity project, the Gold Control school principal and some faculty requested that they become a pilot project school in the second year of the study. They formed an AIC with 10 to 12 faculty and five to nine students in year two with the goal of working with the project team to create a school strategic plan in year two and begin to implement that plan in year three. No parents were ever recruited. The original AIC was led by two faculty members. One leader was paid a stipend, and the other was a volunteer who was working on his own research into academic integrity.

Unique Circumstances

Gold Control serves a wealthy community with an expectation of excellent student performance. In the researcher's opinion, there was genuine enthusiasm for the project by the principal and AIC members at the start of the second year. The AIC began effectively with a broad representation of staff disciplines and student participants. The leader without the stipend appeared to take a more active committee role and created a blog to facilitate communication and an exchange of information within the AIC.

During the first few meetings, the researcher observed a curious disconnect between the AIC and the resource information provided by the project. Similar to the observations at Gold High School, there was very little or no recognition of resources provided by the project that would have helped the AIC sustain progress. The leaders in particular were clearly not reviewing the project notebook and even with researcher prompting, did not utilize the resource. This was observed to lead to questions and discussions during AIC meetings that were uninformed by the resources in the project notebook. Attempts to clarify the availability of resources in the project notebook were met with indifference on the part of the faculty leaders. At the end of the second project year, the AIC had only drafted a revised academic integrity policy for inclusion in its student handbook. This document ultimately failed to advance to the full faculty after AIC members criticized the draft.

The AIC met five times in year two, focusing primarily on rewriting the school's academic integrity policy. AIC members discussed policy language at each board meeting and exchanged draft revisions after each meeting. A final draft rewrite of academic integrity policy was completed near the end of year two with what appeared to be a consensus by the AIC. Two weeks after the last AIC meeting and a day before the draft policy was to be reviewed by the full faculty, an AIC faculty member objected to language in the draft policy. He e-mailed a lengthy critical critique of the draft to the full AIC as well as to the administration. The critique raised issues that could not have been addressed with any expedited rewrite prior to the upcoming faculty meeting. The volunteer AIC teacher leader was incredulous that the AIC member did not communicate these concerns to the AIC in a timely manner to address them before the faculty meeting. This member had been at all the AIC meetings and had not voiced his concerns at the meetings. The principal chose to remove the academic integrity policy review from the faculty agenda the following day.

The internal conflict regarding the policy rewrite led to the resignation of the AIC leader who was receiving the stipend. The second unpaid faculty member, who had been very engaged in the AIC process, became quite discouraged and essentially stopped communicating with the researcher. In follow-up conversations, he would never acknowledge the researcher's goal of sustaining a dialogue. A school vice-principal was assigned to finish the policy rewrite project in year three and then disband the committee with no dialogue about the change of plan offered to the researcher. The committee met only three times in year three, and while maintaining the faculty participation, student involvement dropped to one to three students. The committee finished a draft of a new school policy and disbanded. The school vice-principal, who helped wrap up the committee work, sought to put off the AMIS survey in the spring, but ultimately supported the administration of the survey as defined by the project letter of agreement.

The researcher later learned that another faculty member, a non-AIC member, also was quite open about his dissatisfaction with the work of the AIC.

Apparently this teacher had suggested his own version of an academic integrity policy about two years earlier. That effort did not gain any traction, and he refused to join the current effort. It was noted by students on the AIC that this staff member had encouraged students not to join the committee.

Accomplishments

Gold Control did accomplish a few goals:

- A representative team of students and faculty was recruited to join the AIC
- The AIC used a blog to communicate goals, meeting dates, and narrative for group editing
- A new academic integrity policy was completed and approved by the faculty for inclusion in the student handbook at the end of year three

Reflection

The supposition in this reflection is that the volunteer AIC faculty leader became offended and disengaged with the AIC process after the critical comments of the draft AIC policy by an AIC member and the resignation by his colleague who was receiving the stipend. He would not participate in any meaningful dialogue with the researcher after that event, and the leadership role fell to a vice-principal who had not been an original AIC member. The researcher was told that the vice-principal's task was to wrap up the policy work and disband the committee. This was contrary to the discussions with the principal in year one to begin an AIC in year two, create a strategic plan, and have the AIC become an advocate for academic integrity. As of this writing, no one has volunteered to discuss any further steps to promote academic integrity at the school. It was never clear to the researcher why the faculty member who received the stipend was never fully engaged with the process.

This reflection is offered as a cold dose of reality as to the fragile nature of this type of volunteer school mission. Adversity and criticism can come from many unexpected sources. For any school change process, the support of the administration along with that of committed and resilient school faculty is essential to sustain progress. In the researcher's judgment, there was also a strategic error in providing a stipend to a faculty member who was assigned to lead this effort. That individual never showed the engagement of his volunteer colleague and withdrew when he perceived a conflict. This undoubtedly compounded the sense of frustration by the volunteer AIC leader, who was initially enthusiastic about the project.

Case Study Summary: Cross-Cutting Themes and Fruitful Variations

These case studies are instructive for those interested in replicating the project design with an AIC. There are several themes that were observed in all the schools and some unique observations for individual schools. The study team highlights the following observations for consideration by those seeking to implement their own academic integrity program with an AIC:

- Establish the AIC with the recognition and support of the district administration and with a long-term mission of supporting academic integrity within the school community.
- Identify committed leadership (administration and faculty) who understand that the AIC will face meaningful hurdles and possible opposition.
- Accommodate the AIC leader with extra time (additional planning period, reduced duties, secretarial or competent volunteer support) to plan activities and administer the AIC.
- Maintain regular communication between the principal and AIC leader.
- Appoint an AIC leader with strong team-building and committee facilitation skills or the recognized capacity and desire to develop those skills.
- Appoint an AIC leader with the vision and capacity to develop student and parent leadership on the AIC.
- Facilitate an ongoing educational program for the AIC to understand the best research-based information in support of academic integrity.
- Recognize and highlight the accomplishments of the AIC.

The AIC structure and its support of this project's conceptual model for promoting academic integrity have great potential for application in public and private high schools. In this relatively short implementation study, the study team has observed clear roadblocks to success but also the excellent qualitative outcomes that can result from the work of an effective AIC. The case studies presented here are illustrative of the problems and promise associated with creating an AIC and provide some framework for understanding AIC formation and activities.

———

NOTE

1. Major funding was provided by the John Templeton Foundation, the Richard Davoud Donchian Foundation and Wright Investors' Service. The ideas and opinions expressed in this toolkit are those of the authors and do not necessarily reflect the views of the funders.

Schools Influencing This Book's Academic Integrity Policy

During the spring/summer of 2008, the School for Ethical Education (SEE) completed a search of U.S. public and private school websites that included references to academic integrity/honesty/cheating and/or honor codes or pledges. We specifically searched for schools that represented a broad geographic diversity. There were 93 school websites discovered, which were ultimately sorted down to 33 websites (recognized below) of schools that included definitions of cheating and published integrity policies and/or codes supporting integrity. Of these 33 schools, 18 were public schools and 15 were private schools from a total of 16 states.

We created an outline of a comprehensive academic integrity policy from a review of these 33 schools. We obtained permission from 14 school administrators (bold text in table below) from nine states to include policy narrative or themes and cite their websites to create SEE's synthesis of an academic integrity policy. No single school website contained all of the elements of this policy, and several schools may have contributed concepts to individual themes that were synthesized and paraphrased in this document. Michael Pirhalla served as SEE's intern to complete much of the research to identify these schools.

#	School Name	City	State	Type	URL
1	Academy of the Sacred Heart	New Orleans	LA	Private	www.ashrosary.org
2	Bolles Upper School	Jacksonville	FL	Private	www.bolles.org
3	Booker T Washington High School	Miami	FL	Public	btw.dadeschools.net
4	Cardinal Newman School	Columbia	SC	Private	www.cnhs.org
5	Council Rock High School	Council Rock	PA	Public	www.crsd.org
6	Durham Academy	Durham	NC	Private	www.da.org
7	Edmund Burke High School	Washington	DC	Public	www.eburke.org
8	**Episcopal High School**	Bellaire	TX	Private	www.ehshouston.org/ehs/
9	Girard College High School	Philadelphia	PA	Public	www.girardcollege.org
10	Houston Christian High School	Houston	TX	Private	www.houstonchristianhs.org
11	John Marshall High School	Los Angeles	CA	Public	www.johnmarshallhs.org
12	La Cañada High School	La Cañada	CA	Public	www.lcusd.net/lchs/
13	**Langley High School**	McLean	VA	Public	www.fcps.edu/LangleyHS/
14	**Lexington Catholic High School**	Lexington	KY	Private	www.lexingtoncatholic.com
15	**Mainland Regional High School**	Linwood	NJ	Public	www.mainlandregional.net
16	Maury High School	Norfolk	VA	Public	ww2.nps.k12.va.us/education/school/school.php?sectionid=28
17	McQuaid Jesuit High School	Rochester	NY	Private	www.mcquaid.org
18	**Montclair Kimberley Academy**	Montclair	NJ	Private	www.montclairkimberley.org
19	Montgomery Blair High School	Silver Spring	MD	Public	www.mbhs.edu
20	Monsignor Donovan Catholic High School	Athens	GA	Private	www.mondonhs.com/
21	**Norcross High School**	Norcross	GA	Public	www.norcrosshigh.org
22	**Norfolk Collegiate School**	Norfolk	VA	Private	www.norfolkcollegiate.org
23	**Rabun Gap-Nacoochee School**	Rabun Gap	GA	Public	www.rabungap.org

(continued on next page)

(continued)

24	**Radnor High School**	Radnor	PA	Public	www.rtsd.org/radnorhs/
25	**River Hill High School**	Clarksville	MD	Public	www.howard.k12.md.us/rhhs
26	Spartanburg Day School	Spartanburg	SC	Private	spartanburgdayschool.org
27	St. Francis High School	Alpharetta	GA	Private	www.stfranschool.com
28	**Staples High School**	Westport	CT	Public	shs.westport.k12.ct.us/staples
29	**The Hill School**	Pottstown	PA	Private	www.thehill.org
30	**Woodside High School**	Woodside	CA	Public	www.woodsidehs.org
31	Woodward Academy	College Park	GA	Private	www.woodward.edu
32	William McKinley HS	Honolulu	HI	Public	www.mckinley.k12.hi.us
33	**WT Woodson High School**	Fairfax	VA	Public	www.fcps.edu/woodsonhs

Bibliography

Aaron, R. 1992. "Student Academic Dishonesty: Are Collegiate Institutions Addressing the Issue?" *NASPA* 29 (2): 107–113.

ABC News. 2004. "Cheaters Amok: A Crisis in America's Schools—How It's Done and Why It's Happening." ABC News. Retrieved May 25, 2004, from www.abcnews.com.

Abel, K. 2003. "New Survey: 7 in 10 Teens Admit School Cheating." Retrieved December 31, 2003, from www.familyeducation.com/article/0,1120,1-19468,00.html.

Adams, M. 2005. "Best Practices for Creating and Promoting a Culture That Embraces Integrity in Secondary Schools." Workshop presented at the CAI Fall Conference, Virginia Tech, Blacksburg, VA.

Alschuler, A., and G. Blimling. 1995. "Curbing Epidemic Cheating through Systemic Change." *College Teaching* 43 (4): 123–125.

Aluede, O., E. O. Omoregie, and G. I. Osa-Edoh. 2006. "Academic Dishonesty as a Contemporary Problem in Higher Education: How Academic Advisers Can Help." *Reading Improvement* 43 (2): 97.

Anderman, E. M., T. Griesinger, and G. Westerfield. 1998. "Motivation and Cheating During Early Adolescence." *Journal of Educational Psychology* 90 (1): 84–93.

Anderman, E. M., and C. Midgley. 2004. "Changes in Self-Reported Academic Cheating across the Transition from Middle School to High School." *Contemporary Educational Psychology* 29 (4): 499–517.

Angell, L. R. 2006. "The Relationship of Impulsiveness, Personal Efficacy and Academic Motivation to College Cheating." *College Student Journal* 40 (1): 118–131.

Arce, K. 2001. "Detecting Cheating." Retrieved February 26, 2004, from www.muweb.millersv.edu/~jccomp/acadintegrity/detectingcheating.html.

Associated Press. 2003. "Teachers Caught Cheating on Standardized Tests." Retrieved February 4, 2011, from www.interversity.org/lists/arn-l/archives/Oct2003/msg00375.html.

———. 2007. "Duke's Business School Punishes 34 Graduate Students for Cheating."

———. 2008. "Dude—You Guys Plagiarized an Honor Code?" MSNBC.com, March 30. Retrieved July 20, 2008, from www.msnbc.msn.com/id/23870761/MSN.

Association for Supervision and Curriculum Development. 2004. "Academic Cheating: The Role of Student Self-Efficacy and Identification with School." *Academic Cheating* 2 (23).

Astin, A. W., S. A. Parrott, W. S. Korn, and L. J. Sax. *The American Freshman: Thirty-Year Trends.* Los Angeles: Higher Education Research Institute.

Barnett, D. C., and J. C. Dalton. 1981. "Why College Students Cheat." *Journal of College Student Personnel* 22 (6): 545–551.

Beatty, J. 1997. "For Honor's Sake: Moral Education, Honor Systems, and the Informer Rule." *Educational Theory* 42 (1): 39–50.

Berger, P. 2007. "'Our Sacred Honor': Sadly, Too Few Students Know What It Means." *Education Week.* Available online at www.edweek.org/ew/articles/2007/10/31/10berger.h27.html.

Berges, P. 2005. "The Relationship between Honor Codes and Professional Codes of Conduct." *Integrity Matters: A Journal of Experience and Opinion on Academic Integrity from the Center for Academic Integrity* 1 (1): 6–7.

Bien, E., and S. Bien. 1994. "Democracy as Discipline." National Association of School Psychologists Conference, Seattle, WA, March 2.

Biotech Business Week. 2008. "Bioinformatics: Computer-Based Tool Aids Research, Helps Thwart Questionable Publication Practices." Biotech Business Week (Expanded Reporting): 2195.

Blankenship, K., and B. E. Whitley Jr. 2000. "Relation of General Deviance to Academic Dishonesty." *Ethics & Behavior* 10 (1): 1–12.

Blasi, A. 1980. "Bridging Moral Cognition and Moral Action: A Critical Review of the Literature." *Psychological Bulletin* 88 (1): 1–45.

Bloomfield, B. 2007. "The Uses and Abuses of Honor Codes and Councils." Workshop presented at the Center for Academic Integrity Conference. Christopher Newport University, Newport News, VA.

Bonjean, C., and R. McGee. 1965. "Scholastic Dishonesty among Undergraduates in Differing Systems of Social Control." *Sociology of Education* 38 (2): 127–137.

Bound, J., B. Hershbein, and B. T. Long. 2009. "Playing the Admissions Game: Student Reactions to Increasing College Competition." *Journal of Economic Perspectives* 23 (4): 119–146.

Bracey, G. W. 2005. "Research: A Nation of Cheats." *Phi Delta Kappa* 86 (5): 412.

Broussard, A., and B. Golson. 2000. "High School Honor Code Curbs Cheating." *Education Digest* 65 (6): 27–30.

Bruggerman, E., and K. Hart. 1996. "Cheating, Lying, and Moral Reasoning by Religious and Secular High School Students." *Journal of Educational Research* 89 (6): 340–345.

Bryner, J. 2007. "Do-Gooders Can Become the Worst Cheats; Study: Sense of Moral Superiority Might Lead to Rationalizing Bad Behavior." *LiveScience*, November 15. Available online at www.msnbc.msn.com/id/21820808/wid/11915773?GT1=10613.

Bushway, A., and W. Nash. 1977. "School Cheating Behavior." *Review of Educational Research* 47 (4): 623–632.

Bushweller, K. 1999. "Generation of Cheaters." *American School Board Journal* 186 (4): 24–30, 32.

Calabrese, R., and J. Cochran. 1990. "The Relationship of Alienation to Cheating among a Sample of American Adolescents." *Journal of Research and Development in Education* 23 (2): 65–72.

Callahan, D. 2004a. *The Cheating Culture: Why More Americans Are Doing More to Get Ahead*. Orlando: Harcourt.

———. 2004b. "Education." Retrieved February 19, 2004, from cheatingculture.com/education.

———. 2004c. "Take Back Values." *Nation*, February 9. Retrieved March 18, 2008, from www.thenation.com/doc/20040209/callahan.

———. 2006. "A Better Way to Prevent Student Cheating." *Christian Science Monitor*, May 8. Retrieved February 4, 2011, from www.csmonitor.com/2006/0508/p09s02-coop.html.

Canning, R. 1956. "Does an Honor System Reduce Classroom Cheating? An Experimental Answer." *Journal of Experimental Education* 24 (June): 291–296.

Carroll, C. A. 2004. "Cheating Is Pervasive Problem in Education, Forum Participants Say." *Education Week* 23, no. 24 (February 25): 10.

Carter, S. L., and N. M. Punyanunt-Carter. 2006. "Acceptability of Treatments for Cheating in the College Classroom." *Journal of Instructional Psychology* 33 (3): 212–216.

Center for Academic Integrity. 1999. *Fundamental Values of Academic Integrity*. Durham, NC: Center for Academic Integrity. Retrieved November 24, 2008, from www.academicintegrity.org/fundamental_values_project/index.php.

———. 2007. *Accessing Academic Integrity*. Durham, NC: Center for Academic Integrity.

Character Education Partnership. 2008. *Character Education Quality Standards: A Self-Assessment Tool for Schools and Districts.* Washington, DC: Character Education Partnership.

Chemistry student. 2009. "Multiple Lab Report Plagiarism." Retrieved June 23, 2010, from www.uwindsor.ca/aio/students-true-stories.

Clayton, M. 1999. "School Cheating Up As Stakes Rise." *Christian Science Monitor*, December 14. Retrieved June 30, 2008, from www.csmonitor.com/1999/1214/p1s1.html.

Cobbs, L. 2000. "Honor Codes: Teaching Integrity and Interdependence." In *Student Cheating and Plagiarism in the Internet Era: A Wake-Up Call*, by A. Lathrop and K. Foss, 112–114. Englewood, CO: Libraries Unlimited.

Cochran, J., M. Chamlin, P. Wood, and C. Sellers. 1999. "Shame, Embarrassment, and Formal Sanction Threats: Extending the Deterrence/Rational Choice Model to Academic Dishonesty." *Sociological Inquiry* 69 (1): 92–105.

Coffman, K. 2005. "Institutionalizing and Personalizing a Commitment to Academic Integrity: Reflections of a Student Academic Integrity Board Chairperson." *Integrity Matters: A Journal of Experience and Opinion on Academic Integrity from the Center for Academic Integrity* 1 (1): 1–2.

Coles, R. 1997. *The Moral Intelligence of Children*. New York: Random House.

College Administration Publications. 2000. "New Research on Academic Integrity: The Success of 'Modified' Honor Codes." Retrieved July 9, 2002, from www.collegepubs.com/ref/SFX000515.shtml.

College of William and Mary. 1914. "The Honor System in American Colleges." *William and Mary College Quarterly Historical Magazine* 1: 6–9.

Colson, C. 2000. "Cheating Lessons: Are We Rearing Moral Dunces?" *BreakPoint with Charles Colson*. Retrieved December 31, 2010, from www.breakpoint.org/commentaries/4087-cheating-lessons.

Constitutional Rights Foundation. 2008. "The Cheating Problem." *Bill of Rights in Action* 23 (4): 15–19.

Covington, M. V. 1992. *Making the Grade: A Self-Worth Perspective on Motivation and School Reform*. Cambridge: Cambridge University Press.

Cromwell, S. 2000. "What Can We Do to Curb Student Cheating?" *Education World*, January 24. Retrieved June 30, 2008, from educationworld.com/a_issues/issues068.shtml.

Crown, D. F., and S. M. Spiller. 1998. "Learning from the Literature on Collegiate Cheating: A Review of Empirical Research." *Journal of Business Ethics* 17 (6): 683–700.

Cummings, R., C. D. Maddux, S. Harlow, and L. Dyas. 2002. "Academic Misconduct in Undergraduate Teacher Education Students and Its Relationship to Their Principled Moral Reasoning." *Journal of Educational Psychology* 29 (4): 286–296.

Davis, B. G. 1993. "Preventing Academic Dishonesty." *Tools for Teaching*, 299–312. San Francisco: Jossey-Bass. Retrieved December 31, 2003, from teaching.berkeley.edu/bgd/prevent.html.

Davis, S. F., C. A. Grover, A. H. Becker, and L. N. McGregor. 1992. "Academic Dishonesty: Prevalence, Determinants, Techniques, and Punishments." *Teaching of Psychology* 19 (1): 16.

Dawkins, R. L. 2004. "Attributes and Statuses of College Students Associated with Classroom Cheating on a Small-Sized Campus." *College Student Journal* 38 (1): 116–129.

Delisio, E. R. 2003. "Wire Side Chats: United Against Cheating." *Education World*: 3. Available online at www.educationworld .com/a_issues/chat/chat087.shtml.

——. 2008. "Wire Side Chats: Enlisting Students to Create a Culture of Academic Integrity." *Education World*. Available online at www.educationworld.com/a_issues/chat/chat236/shtml.

Demirjian, K. 2006. "What Is the Price of Plagiarism?" *Christian Science Monitor*. Retrieved December 31, 2010, from www.csmonitor.com/2006/0511/p14s01-lire.html.

DeSena, L. H. 2007. *Preventing Plagiarism: Tips and Techniques*. Urbana, IL: National Council of Teachers of English.

Dunbar, G. 2004. "Schools, Firms Play Role in Teaching Ethics." *Connecticut Post*, April 11: 1.

Educational Test Service and Ad Council. 1999. "Academic Cheating Fact Sheet." Retrieved June 30, 2008, from www.glass-castle.com/clients/www-nocheating-org/adcouncil/research/ cheatingfactsheet.html.

Eisenberg, J. 2004. "To Cheat or Not to Cheat: Effects of Moral Perspective and Situational Variables on Student's Attitudes." *Journal of Moral Education* 33 (2): 163–178.

Ellis, E. D. 1966. "The Honor System Re-examined." *Journal of Higher Education* 37 (8): 459–462.

Ethics Resource Center. 2008. *Ethics Resource Center's National Government Ethics Survey: An Inside View of Public Sector Ethics*. Arlington, VA: Ethics Resource Center.

Evans, E. 1990. "Teacher and Student Perceptions of Academic Cheating in Middle and Senior High Schools." *Journal of Educational Research* 84 (1): 44–52.

Eve, R., and D. Bromley. 1981. "Scholastic Dishonesty among College Undergraduates: Parallel Tests of Two Sociological Explanations." *Youth and Society* 13 (1): 3–22.

Fass, R. 1986. "By Honor Bound: Encouraging Academic Honesty." *Educational Record* 67 (Fall): 32–35.

Feinberg, J. M. 2009. "Perception of Cheaters: The Role of Past and Present Academic Achievement." *Ethics & Behavior* 19 (4): 310–322.

Finn, K. V., and M. R. Frone. 2004. "Academic Performance and Cheating: Moderating Role of School Identification and Self-Efficacy." *Journal of Educational Research* 97 (3): 115–121.

Franklyn-Stokes, A., and S. Newstead. 1995. "Undergraduate Cheating: Who Does What and Why?" *Studies in Higher Education* 20 (2): 159–173.

Gabriel, T. 2010a. "To Stop Cheats, Colleges Learn Their Trickery." *New York Times*, July 5. Retrieved December 31, 2010, from www.nytimes.com/2010/07/06/education/06cheat.html.

——. 2010b. "Plagiarism Lines Blur for Students in Digital Age." *New York Times*, August 1. Retrieved August 2, 2010, from www.msnbc.msn.com/id/38517684/ns/us_news-the_ new_york_times.

Gallant, T. B. 2005. "Promoting Academic Integrity and Transforming Institutional Culture: Self-Study and the Assessment of the Campus Culture of Integrity." Paper presented at the Annual Conference of the Center for Academic Integrity, Virginia Tech, Blacksburg, VA.

Gallant, T. B., and P. Drinan. 2006. "Organizational Theory and Student Cheating: Explanation, Responses, and Strategies." *Journal of Higher Education* 77 (5): 839–860.

Garisto, L. P. 2005. "No Cheating!" *Parents* (November): 231–232.

Gauld, J. W. 2003. "Cheating, Honor Codes and Integrity." *Education Week* 22, no. 29 (April 2): 41.

Geiger, J. R. 1922. "The Honor System in Colleges." *International Journal of Ethics* 32 (4): 398–409.

Gilgoff, D. 2001. "Click on Honorable College Student: Will Computers Make Honor Codes Obsolete?" *US News & World Report*, May 21, 51.

Gilmore, B. 2008. *Plagiarism: Why It Happens and How to Prevent It*. Portsmouth, NH: Heinemann.

Gladwell, M. 2006. "No Mercy: Malcolm Gladwell Questions Zero-Tolerance Programs in Schools." *New Yorker*, September 5, 37.

Goodman, J., and H. Lesnick. 2001. *The Moral Stake in Education: Contested Premises and Practices*. New York: Addison Wesley Longman.

Goodman, J. F. 2005. "How Bad Is Cheating? Taking Dishonesty in the Classroom as Seriously as We Should." *Education Week*: 32, 35.

Gould, D. B. L., and J. J. Roberts 2007. *A Handbook for Developing and Sustaining Honor Systems*. Portland, OR: Council for Spiritual and Ethical Education.

Graham, M., J. Monday, K. O'Brien, and S. Steffen. 1994. "Cheating at Small Colleges: An Examination of Student and Faculty Attitudes and Behaviors." *Journal of College Student Development* 35: 255–260.

Green, S. P. 2002. "Plagiarism, Norms, and the Limits of Theft Law: Some Observations on the Use of Criminal Sanctions in Enforcing Intellectual Property Rights." *Hastings Law Journal* (June 10): 16.

Gross, J. 2003. "Exposing the Cheat Sheet, with the Students' Aid." *New York Times*, November 23.

GSI Teaching and Resource Center. 2007. "Causes and Solutions [Cheating]." Retrieved March 7, 2008, from gsi.berkeley.edu/ resources/conduct/causes.html.

Guttmann, J. 1984. "Cognitive Morality and Cheating Behavior in Religious and Secular School Children." *Journal of Educational Research* 77 (4): 249.

Haines, V. J., G. M. Diekhoff, E. E. LaBeff, and R. E. Clark. 1986. "College Cheating: Immaturity, Lack of Commitment, and the Neutralizing Attitude." *Research in Higher Education* 5: 342–354.

Hall, T., and G. Kuh. 1998. "Honor among Students: Academic Integrity and Honor Codes at State-Assisted Universities." *NASPA Journal* 36 (1): 2–18.

Hansen, R. 1985. "The Crisis of the West Point Honor Code." *Military Affairs* 49 (2): 57–62.

Hard, S. F., J. M. Conway, and A. C. Moran. 2006. "Faculty and College Student Beliefs about the Frequency of Student Academic Misconduct." *Journal of Higher Education* 77 (6): 1058–1080.

Harned, P. J., and K. M. Sutliff. 2004. "Academic Honesty: Teaching Kids Not to Take The Easy Way Out." New Jersey PTA. Retrieved March 15, 2008, from www.njpta.org/committee/chared3.html.

Harris, R. 2001. *Anti-Plagiarism Strategies for Research Papers.* Available online at www.virtualsalt.com/antiplag.htm.

Hartness, E. 2008. "Students' Cheating Scheme Uncovered." WRAL-TV, February 26, 2008. Retrieved July 21, 2010, from www.wral.com/news/local/story/2484284/.

Hecht-Leavitt, L. 2005. "Peer Pressure in High School (Yes, It Can Be a Positive Influence!)." *Integrity Matters: A Journal of Experience and Opinion on Academic Integrity from the Center for Academic Integrity* 1 (1).

Heilbrun, A. B., and M. Georges. 1990. "The Measurement of Principled Morality by the Kohlberg Moral Dilemma Questionnaire." *Journal of Personality Assessment* 55 (1 & 2): 183–194.

Hein, D. 1982. "Rethinking Honor." *Journal of Thought* 17 (1): 3–6.

Hendershott, A., P. Drinan, and M. Cross. 2000. "Toward Enhancing a Culture of Academic Integrity." *NASPA Journal* 37 (4): 587–597.

Heyboer, K. 2003. "Cut-and-Paste, Turn It In—You Call That Cheating?" *Newark Star Ledger*, August 28. Available online at www.nj.com/news/ledger/index.ssf?/base/news-10/1062047712138030.xml.

Hoover, E. 2002. "Honor for Honor's Sake?" *Chronicle of Higher Education*, May 3, A35–A38.

Horacek, D. 2009. "Academic Integrity and Intellectual Autonomy." In *Pedagogy, not Policing: Positive Approaches to Academic Integrity at the University*, edited by T. Twomey, H. White, and K. Sagendorf, 7–17. Syracuse, NY: The Graduate School Press of Syracuse University.

Horowitz, H. 1987. *Campus Life.* New York: Alfred A. Knopf.

Houston, J. 1983. "Kohlberg-Type Moral Instruction and Cheating Behavior." *College Student Journal* 17: 196–204.

Hunter, J. D. 2000. *The Death of Character: Moral Education in an Age without Good or Evil*. New York: Basic Books.

Integritas Project. 2002. "Constitution: The Honor Code of Boston College High School." Retrieved July 14, 2002, from www.fc.bchigh.edu/~integritas.

Isaacson, J. 2004. "College Removes Name of Wal-Mart Heiress on Arena." *Columbia Daily Tribune* via AP in *USA Today*, November 24. Retrieved July 16, 2010, from www.usatoday.com/money/industries/retail/2004-11-24-walmart-heiress-arena_x.htm.

Jarc, R. 2009. "Josephson Institute of Ethics Releases Study on High School Character and Adult Conduct." Retrieved December 16, 2009, from www.josephsoninstitute.org/surveys/index.html.

Jenkins, J., and R. Satterlee. 2005. "Integrity in the Face of Adversity: Building Men and Women of Character in the College Environment." Paper presented at the Center for Academic Integrity International Conference. Virginia Tech, Blacksburg, VA.

Jensen, L. A., J. J. Arnett, S. S. Feldman, and E. Cauffman. 2002. "It's Wrong, but Everybody Does It: Academic Dishonesty among High School and College Students." *Contemporary Educational Psychology* 27 (2): 209–228.

Johnson, G. D., R. Kremer, K. Burke, S. Culbert, B. DeFelice, S. Horton, and P. McKee. 1998. *Sources: Their Use and Acknowledgement*. Dartmouth, NH: Trustees of Dartmouth College.

Johnston, J. 1991. "Reflections on a Moral Dilemma." *Journal of Moral Education* 20 (3): 283–292.

Jordan, A. E. 2001. "College Student Cheating: The Role of Motivation, Perceived Norms, Attitudes, and Knowledge of Institutional Policy." *Ethics & Behavior* 11 (3): 233–247.

Joseph, B. 1997. "For Honor's Sake: Moral Education, Honor Systems, and the Informer Rule." *Educational Theory* 42 (1): 39–50.

Josephson Institute. 2006. *2006 Josephson Institute Report Card on the Ethics of American Youth Part One: Integrity; Summary of Data*. Los Angeles: Josephson Institute of Ethics.

———. 2008. *Josephson Institute's Report Card on American Youth: There's a Hole in Our Moral Ozone and It's Getting Bigger*. Los Angeles: Josephson Institute of Ethics.

———. 2009. *A Study of Values and Behavior concerning Integrity: The Impact of Age, Cynicism and High School Character*. Retrieved on December 13, 2010, from josephsoninstitute.org/surveys/index.html.

Josephson, M., and M. Mertz. 2004. *Changing Cheaters: Promoting Integrity and Preventing Academic Dishonesty*. Los Angeles: Josephson Institute of Ethics.

Karagianis, L. 1999. "The Right Stuff: A Question of Ethics." *MIT Spectrum* (11): 3. Retrieved July 22, 2010, from spectrum.mit.edu/issue/1999-winter/the-right-stuff/.

Keith-Spiegel, P., and B. E. Whitley. 2001. "Introduction to the Special Issue." *Ethics & Behavior* 11 (3): 217–218.

Kendrick, C. 2003. "Talking about Honesty." Retrieved December 31, 2003, from www.familyeducation.com.

Kennedy, R. 2004. "Private Schools: Cheating, an Epidemic." Retrieved April 7, 2004, from www.privateschool.about.com/cs/forteachers/a/cheating_p.htm.

———. 2007. "5 Ways to Prevent Cheating: Gary Niels on Cheating—Part 3: Prevention at School." Retrieved June 25, 2008, from privateschool.about.com/cs/forteachers/a/cheating_4.htm.

Kessler, K. 2003. "Helping High School Students Understand Academic Integrity." *English Journal* 96 (6): 56–63.

Kibler, W. L. 1993. "A Framework for Addressing Academic Dishonesty from a Student Development Perspective." *NASPA Journal* 31 (1): 8–18.

———. 1994. "Addressing Academic Dishonesty: What Are Institutions of Higher Education Doing and Not Doing?" *NASPA Journal* 31 (2): 92–101.

Kibler, W. L., E. M. Nuss, B. G. Paterson, and G. Pavela. 1988. *Academic Integrity and Student Development: Legal Issues, Policy Perspectives*. Asheville, NC: College Administration Publications.

Kleiner, C., and M. Lord. 1999. "The Cheating Game: 'Everyone's Doing It,' from Grade School to Graduate School." *US News & World Report*, November 22. Retrieved February 19, 2004, from www.usnewsclassroom.com.

Koch, K. 2000. "Cheating in Schools." *CQ Researcher* 10 (32). Retrieved September 14, 2002, from library.cqpress.com.

Kohlberg, L. 1969. "Stage and Sequence: The Cognitive-Developmental Approach to Socialization." In *Handbook of Socialization Theory and Research*, edited by D. A. Goslin, 347–380. Chicago: Rand McNally.

Kuh, G. D., and S. Hu. 1999. "Unraveling the Complexity of the Increase in College Grades from the Mid-1980s to the Mid-1990s." *Educational Evaluation and Policy Analysis* 21: 297–320.

LaBeff, E., R. Clark, V. Haines, and G. Diekhoff. 1990. "Situational Ethics and College Student Cheating." *Sociological Inquiry* 60 (2): 190–198.

Labi, A. 2007. "Corrupt Schools, Corrupt Universities, What Can Be Done: Corruption in Education Is Growing Worldwide, UNESCO Reports." *Chronicle of Higher Education* 53 (41): 43.

Lathrop, A., and K. Foss. 2000. *Student Cheating and Plagiarism in the Internet Era: A Wake-Up Call*. Englewood, CO: Greenwood.

———. 2005. *Guiding Students from Cheating and Plagiarism to Honesty and Integrity: Strategies for Change*. Westport, CT: Libraries Unlimited.

Le Conte Stevens, W. 1906. "The Honor System in American Colleges." *Popular Science*. 68: 176–185.

Lee, R. G., and L. M. Burns. 2005. "25 Ways to Jumpstart Plagiarism Discussion in Your Class." Paper presented at the International Conference of the Center for Academic Integrity. Quinnipiac University, Hamden, CT.

Leland, B. H. 2002. "Plagiarism and the Web" (January 29). Retrieved December 31, 2010, from www.wiu.edu/users/mfbhl/wiu/plagiarism.htm.

Leming, J. 1978. "Cheating Behavior, Situational Influence, and Moral Development." *Journal of Educational Research* (71): 214–217.

———. 1980. "Cheating Behavior, Subject Variables, and Components of the Internal-External Scale under High and Low Risk Conditions." *Journal of Educational Research* 74 (2): 83–87.

Lickona, T. 1991. *Educating for Character: How Our Schools Can Teach Respect and Responsibility*. New York: Bantam Books.

Lickona, T., and M. Davidson. 2005. *Smart & Good High Schools: Integrating Excellence and Ethics for Success in School, Work, and Beyond*. Cortland, NY, and Washington, DC: Center for the 4th & 5th Rs and Character Education Partnership.

Little, M. T. 2002. "Towards the Improved Efficacy of the Lovett School's Honor Code." *Education*. Master's thesis, Georgia State University, Atlanta, GA, 75.

Lovett-Hooper, G., M. Komarraju, R. Weston, and S. Dollinger. 2007. "Is Plagiarism a Forerunner of Other Deviance? Imagined Futures of Academically Dishonest Students." *Ethics & Behavior* 17 (3): 323–326.

Lovett, B. J. 2009. "The Science of Cheating." In *Pedagogy, not Policing: Positive Approaches to Academic Integrity at the University*, edited by T. Twomey, H. White, and K. Sagendorf, 43–48. Syracuse, NY: Graduate School Press of Syracuse University.

Lucas, G. M., and J. Friedrich. 2005. "Individual Differences in Workplace Deviance and Integrity as Predictors of Academic Dishonesty." *Ethics & Behavior* 15 (1): 15–35.

Ludeman, R. B. 1988. "A Survey of Academic Integrity Practices in U.S. Higher Education." *Journal of College Student Development* 29 (March): 172–173.

MacDonald, J. 2004. "Lying: If You Play by the Rules Will You Lose Out? Many Americans Think So." *Christian Science Monitor,* June 23. Retrieved June 23, 2004, from www.csmonitor.com.

Malinoski, C. I., and C. P. Smith. 1985. "Moral Reasoning and Moral Conduct: An Investigation Prompted by Kohlberg's Theory." *Journal of Personality and Social Psychology* 49 (4): 1016–1027.

Mathews, C. O. 1932. "The Honor System." *Journal of Higher Education* 3 (8): 411–415.

Mathews, J. 2001. "Students Can Often Cheat Their Punishment." *Washington Post*, October 28, A01.

May, K., and B. Loyd. 1993. "Academic Dishonesty: The Honor System and Students' Attitudes." *Journal of College Student Development* 34 (March): 125–129.

McCabe, D. 1992. "The Influence of Situational Ethics on Cheating among College Students." *Sociological Inquiry* 62 (3): 365–374.

———. 1993. "Faculty Responses to Academic Dishonesty: The Influence of Student Honor Codes." *Research in Higher Education* 34 (5): 647–658.

———. 1999. "Academic Dishonesty among High School Students." *Adolescence* 34 (136): 681–687.

———. 2005. "It Takes a Village: Academic Dishonesty and Educational Opportunity." *Liberal Education* 91 (3): 26–31.

McCabe, D. L., and W. J. Bowers. 1994. "Academic Dishonesty among Males in College: A Thirty-Year Perspective." *Journal of College Student Development* 35 (1): 5–10.

McCabe, D., and G. Pavela. 1997. "The Principled Pursuit of Academic Integrity." *AAHE Bulletin* 50: 11–12.

———. 2000. "Some Good News about Academic Integrity." *Change* 32: 32–38.

McCabe, D., and J. M. Stephens. 2006. "'Epidemic' as Opportunity: Internet Plagiarism as a Lever for Cultural Change." *Teachers College Record,* November 30. Retrieved September 19, 2009, from www.tcrecord.org/content.asp?contentid=12860.

McCabe, D., and L. K. Trevino. 1993. "Academic Dishonesty: Honor Codes and Other Contextual Influences." *Journal of Higher Education* 64 (5): 522–538.

———. 1996. "What We Know about Cheating in College." *Change* 28 (1): 28–33.

———. 1997. "Individual and Contextual Influence on Academic Dishonesty: A Multicampus Investigation." *Research in Higher Education* 38 (3): 379–396.

———. 2002. "Honor Codes and Other Contextual Influences on Academic Integrity: A Replication and Extension to Modified Honor Code Settings." *Research in Higher Education* 43 (3): 357–378.

McCabe, D., L. K. Trevino, and K. Butterfield. 1999. "Academic Integrity in Honor Code and Non-Honor Code Environments: A Qualitative Investigation." *Journal of Higher Education* 70 (2): 211–234.

———. 2001a. "Cheating in Academic Institutions: A Decade of Research." *Ethics & Behavior* 11 (3): 219–232.

——. 2001b. "Dishonesty in Academic Environments: The Influence of Peer Reporting Requirements." *Journal of Higher Education* 72 (1): 29–45.

McLaughlin, R., and S. Ross. 1989. "Student Cheating in High School: A Case of Moral Reasoning vs. 'Fuzzy Logic.'" *High School Journal* 72 (February/March): 97–104.

McMurtry, K. 2001. "E-Cheating: Combating a 21st Century Challenge." *T H E Journal* 29 (40): 36–41.

Menager-Beeley, R., and L. Paulos. 2006. *Understanding Plagiarism: A Student Guide to Writing Your Own Work.* Boston: Houghton Mifflin.

Michaels, J., and T. Miethe. 1989. "Applying Theories of Deviance to Academic Cheating." *Social Science Quarterly* 70 (4): 870–885.

Modenbach, K. 2003. "Curb Cheating with Prevention Strategies." *Education World*, October 27. Retrieved December 31, 2010, from www.educationworld.com/a_curr/voice/voice099.shtml.

Montor, K. 1971. "Cheating in High School." *School and Society* 99 (February): 96–98.

Mouberry, A. 2004. "Critical Transitions: An Analysis of Students' Perceptions, Attitudes and Behaviors Related to Academic Integrity During the Transition from High School to College." Available online at www.academicintegrity.org/cai_research/templeton_mouberry.php

Muha, D. 2003. "New Study Confirms Internet Plagiarism Is Prevalent." Rutgers: The State University of New Jersey. Available online at ur.rutgers.edu/medrel/viewArticle.html?%20ArticleID=3408.

Murdock, T. B., and E. M. Anderman. 2006. "Motivational Perspectives on Student Cheating: Toward an Integrated Model of Academic Dishonesty." *Educational Psychologist* 41 (3): 129–145.

Murdock, T. B., N. M. Hale, and M. Weber. 2001. "Predictors of Cheating among Early Adolescents: Academic and Social Motivations." *Contemporary Educational Psychology* 26 (1): 96–115.

Murdock, T. B., A. Miller, and J. Kohlhardt. 2004. "Effects of Classroom Context Variables on High School Students' Judgments of the Acceptability and Likelihood of Cheating." *Journal of Educational Psychology* 96 (4): 765–777.

Murdock, T. B., and J. M. Stephens. 2006. "Is Cheating Wrong? Students' Reasoning about Academic Dishonesty." In *The Psychology of Academic Cheating*, edited by E. M. Anderman and T. B. Murdock, 229–251. New York: Elsevier.

Nelsen, E. A., R. Grinder, and M. Mutterer. 1969. "Sources of Variance in Behavioral Measures of Honesty in Temptation Situations: Methodological Analyses." *Developmental Psychology* 1 (3): 265–279.

Nelson, T. R. 2004. "How Do Your Work Ethics Measure Up?" *Christian Science Monitor*, March 3. Available online at www.csmonitor.com.

Newman, A. M. 2004. "Is Your Child a Cheater?" MSN.com. Retrieved September 17, 2004, from www.msn.com.

Newstead, S. E., A. Franklyn-Stokes, and P. Armstead. 2002. "Individual Differences in Student Cheating." *Journal of Educational Psychology* 88 (2): 229–241.

Newton, J. 2001. "Plagiarism and the Challenges of Essay Writing: Learning from Our Students." In *Voices from the Classroom: Reflections on Teaching and Learning in Higher Education*, edited by J. Newton, J. Ginsburg, J. Rehner, P. Rogers, S. Sbrizzi, and J. Spencer. Toronto: University of Toronto Press.

Niels, G. 1996. *Is the Honor Code a Solution to the Cheating Epidemic?* New York: Esther A. and Joseph Klingenstein Center for Independent School Education, Columbia University.

Parr, F. W. 1936. "The Problem of Student Honesty." *Journal of Higher Education* 7 (6): 318–326.

Pavela, G., and D. McCabe. 1993. "The Surprising Return of Honor Codes." *Planning for Higher Education* 21 (Summer): 27–32.

PBS Kids. 2002. "Cheating." Retrieved December 3, 2003, from www.pbskids.org/itsmylife/school/cheating/you_said_it.html.

Pearlin, L., M. R. Yarrow, and H. Scarr. 1967. "Unintended Effects of Parental Aspirations: The Case of Children's Cheating." *American Journal of Sociology* 73 (1): 73–83.

People Magazine. 2002. "Cheat Wave." *People*, June 17. Retrieved July 27, 2010, from www.sabri.org/cheatwave.htm.

Petress, K. C. 2003. "Academic Dishonesty: A Plague on Our Profession." *Education* 123 (3): 624–627.

Plagiarism dot Org. 2009. "Types of Plagiarism." Retrieved August 11, 2009, from www.plagiarism.org/plag_article_types_of_plagiarism.html.

Pope, D. C. 2001. *Doing School: How We Are Creating a Generation of Stressed Out, Materialistic, and Miseducated Students.* New Haven: Yale University Press.

Princeton University. 2008. "Academic Integrity at Princeton." Princeton, Office of the Dean of the College.

Puka, B. 2005. "Student Cheating: As Serious an Academic Integrity Problem as Faculty-Administration Business as Usual?" *Liberal Education* 91 (3): 32.

Read, B. 2008. "Anti-Cheating Crusader Vexes Some Professors." *Chronicle of Higher Education* 54 (25): 1.

Reilly, P. 2008. "Integrity, Stories, and Deliberateness." Retrieved August 4, 2009, from preilly.wordpress.com/2008/11/15/integrity-stories-and-deliberateness/

Reimer, J., D. P. Paolitto, and R. Hersh. 1979. *Promoting Moral Growth: From Piaget to Kohlberg.* New York: Longman.

Rest, J. R., D. Narvaez, M. Bebeau, and S. Thoma. 1999. *Postconventional Moral Thinking: A Neo-Kohlbergian Approach.* Mahwah, NJ: Erlbaum.

Riera, M., and J. D. Prisco. 2004. "Your Cheating Part: An Opportunity to Teach Kids about Integrity." *Our Children* 28 (1): 8–9.

Roberts, D., and W. Rabinowitz. 1992. "An Investigation of Student Perceptions of Cheating in Academic Situations." *Review of Higher Education* 15 (2): 179–190.

Robinson, E., R. Amburgey, E. Swank, and C. Faulkner. 2004. "Test Cheating in a Rural College: Studying the Importance of Individual and Situational Factors." *College Student Journal* 38 (3): 380–395.

Roffey, A., and D. Porter. 1992. "Moral Decision Making and Nontoleration of Honor Code Offenses." *Counseling and Values* 36 (2): 135–150.

Roig, M., 2001. "Plagiarism and Paraphrasing Criteria of College and University Professors." *Ethics & Behavior* 11 (3): 307–323.

Roig, M., and C. Ballew. 1994. "Attitudes toward Cheating of Self and Others by College Students and Professors." *Psychological Record* 44 (1): 3–12.

Roig, M., and A. Marks. 2006. "Attitudes toward Cheating Before and After the Implementation of a Modified Honor Code: A Case Study." *Ethics & Behavior* 16 (2): 163–171.

Rojstaczer, S. 2010. *Grade Inflation at America's Colleges and Institutions.* Retrieved June 15, 2010, from www.gradeinflation .com.

Roth, N., and D. McCabe. 1995. "Communication Strategies for Addressing Academic Dishonesty." *Journal of College Student Development* 36 (6): 531–541.

Rudolph, F. 1962. *The American College and University: A History.* New York: Alfred A, Knopf.

Scanlon, P. M. 2003. "Student Online Plagiarism: How Do We Respond?" *College Teaching* 51: 161–164.

Schab, F. 1991. "Schooling without Learning: Thirty Years of Cheating in High School." *Adolescence* 26 (102): 839–848.

Scott, F. 2004. "The Truth about Lying." Retrieved December 31, 2010, from www2.scholastic.com/browse/article.jsp?id=702.

Seeman, H. 2003. "Cheating in the Classroom: How to Prevent It (and How to Handle It if It Happens)." Retrieved April 7, 2004, from www.education-world.com.

Sergiovanni, T. J. 1996. *Leadership for the Schoolhouse.* San Francisco: Jossey-Bass.

Shelton, J., and J. Hill. 1969. "Effects on Cheating of Achievement Anxiety and Knowledge of Peer Performance." *Developmental Psychology* 1 (5): 449–455.

Shore, K. 2003. "Ken Shore's Classroom Problem Solver: Prevent Cheating." Retrieved April 7, 2004, from www.educationworld. com/a_curr/shore/shore022.shtml.

Singhal, A., and P. Johnson. 1983. "How to Halt Student Dishonesty." *College Student Journal* 17: 13–19.

Sisti, D. A. 2004. "Moral Slippage: How Do High School Students 'Justify' Internet Plagiarism?" Retrieved December 31, 2010, from www.academicintegrity.org/cai_research/templeton_ sisti.php.

Slobogin, K. 2002. "Survey: Many Students Say Cheating's OK; Confessed Cheater: 'What's Important Is Getting Ahead.'" CNN, April 5. Retrieved February 19, 2004, from www.cnn. com.

Snyder, S. 2003. "Schools Using a New Force to Combat Cheating: Students." *Philadelphia Inquirer*, January 29. Retrieved February 4, 2011 from articles.philly.com/2003-01-29/ news/25466681_1_cheating-students-academic-integrity.

Staats, S., J. M. Hupp, H. Wallace, and J. Gresley. 2009. "Heroes Don't Cheat: An Examination of Academic Dishonesty and Students' Views on Why Professors Don't Report Cheating." *Ethics & Behavior* 19 (3): 14.

Standler, R. B. 2000. "Plagiarism in Colleges in USA." (Updated February 3, 2007.) Retrieved March 7, 2008, from www.rbs2 .com/plag.htm.

Stannard, C., and W. Bowers. 1970. "The College Fraternity as an Opportunity Structure for Meeting Academic Demands." *Social Problems* 17 (Summer/Spring): 371–390.

Starkey, L. J. 2007. "Measuring Progress in Academic Integrity Promotion: A Checklist Approach Facilitates Institutional Review of Policies, Practices and Communications." Newport, VA: Center for Academic Integrity.

Stearns, S. A. 2001. "The Student-Instructor Relationship's Effect on Academic Integrity." *Ethics & Behavior* 11 (3): 275–285.

Stenmark, C. K., A. L. Antes, X. Wang, J. J. Caughron, C. E. Thiel, and M. D. Mumford. 2010. "Strategies in Forecasting Outcomes in Ethical Decision-Making: Identifying and Analyzing the Causes of the Problem." *Ethics & Behavior* 20 (2): 110–127.

Stephens, J. M. 2004. "Psychology through Ecology: Academic Motivation, Moral Aptitudes, and Cheating Behavior in Middle and High School Settings." *Educational Psychology*, Stanford University. Retrieved on December 10, 2009, from www.academicintegrity.org/cai_research/templeton_stephens .php.

———. 2005. "Justice or Just Us? What to Do about Cheating." In *Guiding Students from Cheating and Plagiarism to Honesty and Integrity: Strategies for Change*, edited by A. Lanthrop and K. Foss, 32–34. Westport, CT: Libraries Unlimited.

———. 2007. "Cheating." *Encyclopedia of Educational Psychology*. Thousand Oaks, CA: Sage Press.

Stephens, J. M., and H. Gehlbach. 2006. "Under Pressure and Underengaged: Motivational Profiles and Academic Cheating in High School." In *The Psychology of Academic Cheating*, edited by E. M. Anderman and T. B. Murdock, 107–140. New York: Elsevier.

Stephens, J. M., and R. W. Roeser. 2003. "Quantity of Motivation and Qualities of Classrooms: A Person-Centered Comparative Analysis of Cheating in High School." Meeting of the American Educational Research Association. Chicago, IL.

Stephens, J. M., and D. B. Wangaard. 2010. *Preliminary Data Analysis of New England Public High School Students Responses to Attitudes, Motivation and Integrity Survey.* Milford, CT: The School for Ethical Education.

Stephens, J. M., M. F. Young, and T. Calabrese. 2007. "Does Moral Judgment Go Offline When Students Are Online? A Comparative Analysis of Undergraduates' Beliefs and Behaviors Related to Conventional and Digital Cheating." *Ethics & Behavior* 17 (3): 233–544.

Stern, L. 2007. *What Every Student Should Know about Avoiding Plagiarism.* New York: Pearson Longman.

Sternberg, R. J. 2009. "Liars, Cheats, & Scoundrels . . . and What to Do about Them." *Tufts* magazine (17) 1: 28–31.

Stokes, F. 1995. "Undergraduate Cheating: Who Does What and Why?" *Studies in Higher Education* 20 (2): 159–173.

Stricherz, M. 2001. "Many Teachers Ignore Cheating, Survey Finds." *Education Week*, May 9. Available online at www.edweek.org/ ew/articles/2001/05/09/34cheat.h20.html.

Strom, R. D., and P. S. Strom. 2005. "Cheating in Schools." Child Research Net. Retrieved July 22, 2008, from www.child research.net/RESOURCE/RESEARCH/2005/STROM.HTM.

Sussman, D. 2003. "Academic Integrity? ABCNEWS Primetime Poll: Cheating Among Teens Common, Effective." ABC News. Retrieved May 25, 2004, from www.abcnews.com.

Syer, C. A., and B. M. Shore. 2001. "Science Fairs: What Are the Sources of Help for Students and How Prevalent Is Cheating?" *School Science and Mathematics* 101 (4): 206–220.

Taylor, B. 2004. "Donna Andrews: A Profile in Integrity." Des Plaines, IL: Oakton Community College.

———. n.d. "Academic Integrity: A Letter to My Students." Des Plaines, IL: Oakton Community College.

Teel Institute. 1998. *Moral Classrooms: The Development of Character and Integrity in the Elementary School.* Kansas City, MO: Teel Institute for the Development of Integrity and Ethical Behavior.

Thompson, A., and A. Levine. 2005. "How Do You Educate Students about the Honor Principle When Your Peers Don't Even Know That Such a Principle Exists?" Workshop presented at the CAI Conference, Virginia Tech, Blacksburg, VA.

Thorpe, M. F., D. J. Pittenger, and B. D. Reed. 1999. "Cheating the Researcher: A Study of the Relation between Personality Measures and Self-Reported Cheating." *College Student Journal* 33 (1): 49.

Throckmorton-Belzer, L., P. Keith-Spiegel, and J. Wrangham. 2001. "Student Response to a Collective Penalty for Reported Cheating: A Case Study." Special issue, *Ethics & Behavior* 11 (3): 343–348.

Tittle, C., and A. S. Rower. 1973. "Moral Appeal, Sanction Threat, and Deviance: An Experimental Test." *Social Problems* 20 (4): 488–498.

Treadaway, D. 2002. "Increased Resources, Education Recommended to Improve Academic Integrity on Campus." *Whistle.* Atlanta: Georgia Institute of Technology.

Tucker, N. B. 1909. "The Honor System at William and Mary College." *William and Mary College Quarterly Historical Magazine* 18: 165–171.

Twomey, T., H. White, and K. Sagendorf, eds. 2009. *Pedagogy, not Policing: Positive Approaches to Academic Integrity at the University.* Syracuse, NY: Graduate School Press of Syracuse University.

U.S. Copyright Office. 2007. *Subject Matter and Scope of Copyright.* Washington, DC: U.S. Copyright Office.

———. 2008. *Copyright Basics.* Washington, DC: Library of Congress.

———. 2009. *Fair Use.* Washington, DC: Library of Congress.

US Legal, Inc. 2008. "Plagiarism Law and Legal Definition." Retrieved August 11, 2009, from definitions.uslegal.com/p/plagiarism/.

US News and World Report. 1999. "Exclusive Poll: Cheaters Win." *US News & World Report,* November 13.

U.S. Office of Science and Technology. 2000. *Federal Research Misconduct Policy.* Washington, DC: U.S. Office of Science and Technology. Available online at ori.hhs.gov/policies/fed_research_misconduct.shtml.

Vencat, E. F., J. Overdorf, and J. Adams. 2006. "The Perfect Score: Student Cheating Is Reaching New Levels, Forcing an Overhaul of Standardized Tests." *Newsweek,* March 27, 3.

Viadero, D. 2008. "Project Probes Digital Media's Effect on Ethics: Howard Gardner Leads Team Studying Youths' Web Norms." *Education Week* 28 (13): 1, 12.

Villano, M. 2006. "Taking the Work out of Homework: With the Rise of the Internet, Schools Are Seeing an Epidemic of Cut-and-Paste Plagiarism, but the Same Technology That's Making Plagiarism Easy Is Being Used by Teachers to Catch Copycats in the Act." *T H E Journal* 33 (15): 24–30.

Vinski, E. J., and G. S. Tryon. 2009. "Study of Cognitive Dissonance Intervention to Address High School Students' Cheating Attitudes and Behaviors." *Ethics & Behavior* 19 (3): 218–226.

Vitro, F., and L. Schoer. 1972. "The Effects of Probability of Test Success, Test Importance, and Risk of Detection on the Incidence of Cheating." *Journal of School Psychology* 10 (3): 269–277.

Wangaard, D. B. 2006. *The Golden Compass for Character-Based Decision Making.* Boone, NC: Character Development Group.

Wangaard, D. B., and R. Parisi. 2008. *Lindbergh School District National School of Character Site-Visit Report.* Washington, DC: Character Education Partnership, 5.

Wangaard, D. B., and J. M. Stephens. 2006. "Justification for Implementing and Evaluating a Pilot Academic Integrity Program." The School for Ethical Education. Retrieved January 26, 2008, from www.ethicsed.org/programs/integrity-works/justification.htm.

———. 2009. *Building Moral Character through Academic Integrity: Project Update Number 8.* Milford, CT: The School for Ethical Education.

Ward, D., and W. Beck 1990. "Gender and Dishonesty." *Journal of Social Psychology* 130 (3): 333–339.

Warren, K. 2004. *Erasuregate: The Rise and Fall of Roger Previs and Stratfield School.* New Haven, CT: Hopkins School.

Welter, T. 2008. "Ask about Cheating in School and the Stories Pour Out." *Orange County Register,* February 29. Retrieved July 21, 2010, from www.ocregister.com/articles/cheating-109834-tests-cheatinginschool.html.

Whitley, B. E., and P. Keith-Spiegel. 2001. *Academic Integrity as an Institutional Issue.* Muncie, IN: Department of Psychological Science, Ball State University, 325–342.

———. 2002. *Academic Dishonesty: An Educator's Guide.* Mahwah, NJ: Lawrence Erlbaum.

Whitley, B. E. J., A. B. Nelson, and C. J. Jones. 1999. "Gender Differences in Cheating Attitudes and Classroom Cheating Behavior: A Meta-Analysis." *Sex Roles: A Journal of Research* 41 (9–10): 657–680.

Who's Who among American High School Students. 1998. "Cheating and Succeeding: Record Numbers of Top Ten School Students Take Ethical Shortcuts." Retrieved May 26, 2004, from www.whoswho-teachers.com/3attitudesANDopinions/29.aspx.

Wilgoren, J. 2002. "School Cheating Scandal Tests a Town's Values." *New York Times,* February 14. Retrieved July 27, 2010, from www.nytimes.com/2002/02/14/us/school-cheating-scandal-tests-a-town-s-values.html.

Wowra, S. A. 2007a. "Academic Dishonesty: Introduction to the Special Issue." *Ethics & Behavior* 17 (3): 211–214.

———. 2007b. "Moral Identities, Social Anxiety, and Academic Dishonesty among American College Students." *Ethics & Behavior* 17 (3): 303–321.

Index

Acknowledgments

Though only two names appear on the cover of this book, its development and publication would not have been possible without the support of many others. We are especially grateful to students, faculty, and staff at the high schools involved in our *Achieving with Integrity* project. Many of the ideas and activities included in this toolkit are products of their imaginations and perseverance, and we are forever thankful for their creativity and commitment to integrity. Of course, the project itself would have been a non-starter if not for the financial support of Wright Investors' Service, the John Templeton Foundation, and the Richard Davoud Donchian Foundation. While the ideas expressed in this book do not necessarily reflect their views, our project would not have been possible without their remarkable commitment to promote character education and young people's moral development. Finally, we would like to thank Sandi Michaelson for her encouragement of the concept of this toolkit, Michael Pirhalla for his professional contributions as an intern, Maryann Betts for her careful reading of the draft, and Karl Anderson at Search Institute for his clear editorial oversight.

DBW, JMS

About the Authors

David B. Wangaard, Ed.D., is the director of the School for Ethical Education in Milford, CT. Prior to earning his doctorate in Educational Leadership from the University of Northern Colorado, David was a school principal in Alaska. He developed the Integrity Works! project at SEE to help secondary schools initiate academic integrity programs.

Jason M. Stephens, Ph.D., is an assistant professor in the Department of Educational Psychology at the University of Connecticut, where he teaches classes on human learning and academic motivation. His research focuses on academic motivation and moral development during adolescence, particularly as they relate to the problem of academic dishonesty.

DATE DUE
